# Generally Speaking

# Generally Speaking

*An Invitation to Concept-Driven
Sociology*

EVIATAR ZERUBAVEL

# OXFORD
## UNIVERSITY PRESS

Oxford University Press is a department of the University of Oxford. It furthers the University's objective of excellence in research, scholarship, and education by publishing worldwide. Oxford is a registered trade mark of Oxford University Press in the UK and certain other countries.

Published in the United States of America by Oxford University Press
198 Madison Avenue, New York, NY 10016, United States of America.

Library of Congress Cataloging-in-Publication Data
Names: Zerubavel, Eviatar, author.
Title: Generally speaking : an invitation to concept-driven sociology / Eviatar Zerubavel.
Description: New York, NY : Oxford University Press, [2021] | Includes bibliographical references and index.
Identifiers: LCCN 2020017672 (print) | LCCN 2020017673 (ebook) | ISBN 9780197519271 (hardback) | ISBN 9780197519288 (paperback) | ISBN 9780197519301 (epub)
Subjects: LCSH: Sociology—Methodology.
Classification: LCC HM511 .Z47 2021 (print) | LCC HM511 (ebook) | DDC 301.01—dc23
LC record available at https://lccn.loc.gov/2020017672
LC ebook record available at https://lccn.loc.gov/2020017673

1 3 5 7 9 8 6 4 2

Paperback printed by LSC Communications, United States of America
Hardback printed by Bridgeport National Bindery, Inc., United States of America

*To my terrific students,*

*who "carry the torch"*

# Contents

*Preface*                                                        ix

1. **Focusing**                                                   1
   A Concept-Driven Sociology                                     1
   The Focused Mind                                               7
   Attentional Socialization                                     11

2. **Generalizing**                                              13
   A Generic Sociology                                           13
   Transcontextual Research                                      17
   Theorizing Generically                                        19

3. **Exampling**                                                 23
   Contextual Diversity                                          24
   Cultural and Historical Diversity                             29
   Situational Diversity                                         31
   Multilevel Research                                           35

4. **Analogizing**                                               37
   The Analogical Imagination                                    37
   Cross-Cultural Analogizing                                    43
   Cross-Historical Analogizing                                  47
   Cross-Domain Analogizing                                      49
   Cross-Level Analogizing                                       57

5. **Eureka!**                                                    59
   From "No-Nos" to Methodological Virtues                       59
   Analogical Transfers                                          64
   Diving Beneath the Social Surface                             70

*Notes*                                                          73
*Bibliography*                                                   87
*Author Index*                                                  101
*Subject Index*                                                 105

# Preface

I started practicing a "concept-driven" brand of sociology already as a graduate student in the 1970s, initially articulating the theoretico-methodological implications of doing so in "If Simmel Were a Fieldworker: On Formal Sociological Theory and Analytical Field Research," a paper I presented at the 1977 meeting of the Eastern Sociological Society and published three years later as an article. I later expanded such a sociology to also include a "generic" and therefore transcontextual component in my books *The Fine Line* (1991) and *Time Maps* (2003), following which I was urged by my then-students Asia Friedman and Thomas DeGloma to explicitly spell out how I actually produced those books, which led to "Generally Speaking: The Logic and Mechanics of Social Pattern Analysis," a paper I presented at the 2004 meeting of the American Sociological Association and published three years later as an article.

Four intellectual-stylistically similar books (*The Elephant in the Room, Ancestors and Relatives, Hidden in Plain Sight,* and *Taken for Granted*) later, I felt ready to write a book specifically addressing this common yet effectively unarticulated theoretico-methodological thread in my work. It was at that point that I was actually approached by my Oxford University Press editor James Cook to do in fact just that, and on November 10, 2017, I finally started writing this book.

I am particularly indebted to Yael Zerubavel, Iddo Tavory, Asia Friedman, Tom DeGloma, Wayne Brekhus, Steph Peña-Alves, Tali Jaffe-Dax, Tzipy Lazar-Shoef, and Natalia Ruiz-Junco, who read several early versions of this book and spent many hours discussing them with me. I also benefited tremendously from the very helpful comments I received from Lynn Chancer, Kai Erikson, Ira Cohen, Paul McLean, Gabrielle Martin, Lexi Gervis, Johanna Foster, Jamie Mullaney, John Levi Martin, and Lisa Campion on a preliminary draft.

East Brunswick, New Jersey, 2020

# 1

# Focusing

In the fields of observation chance favors only the mind
which is prepared.

—Louis Pasteur, quoted in Richard M. Pearce,
"Chance and the Prepared Mind," 941

One of the very first things sociology students do is take "Research
Methods," a required course specifically designed to introduce them
to various different methodological approaches to how to conduct
sociological research. The present book is an attempt to introduce
another such approach that has yet to be explicitly articulated.

Forty-nine years and twelve books after deciding to become a
sociologist, I am actually ready to reflect on the methodological
underpinnings of my work, and in particular on how I view the
complex and so often contested relation between social "theorizing"
and social "research."[1] This book is the product of my effort to do so.

## A Concept-Driven Sociology

As so glaringly evidenced in the artificial curricular split between
"theory" and "methods" courses in many sociology programs, the
conventional distinction between "theory" and "methodology" is
highly exaggerated. Indeed, in the spirit of Emile Durkheim, who
masterfully integrates the two in *The Rules of Sociological Method*,[2]
I actually consider it a false distinction.[3] Throughout this book

*Generally Speaking*. Eviatar Zerubavel, Oxford University Press (2021). © Oxford University Press.
DOI: 10.1093/oso/9780197519271.001.0001.

I therefore use the hyphenated term *theoretico-methodological* to convey their actual inseparability from each other.

There are two effectively antithetical approaches to conducting sociological research, the significance of the distinction between which by far exceeds that of the conventional one between so-called quantitative and qualitative epistemologies. On the one hand there is the *data-driven* approach, where projects begin with the researcher identifying a particular set of data associated with a particular social setting (a neighborhood, a school), group (a family, an organization), or event (an election, a strike). On the other hand there is the *theory-driven* approach, in which they begin with a particular "theory." As Michael Burawoy, for example, puts it,

> *We don't start with data, we start with theory.* Without theory we are blind—we cannot see the world. Theory is the necessary lens that we bring to our relationship to the world and thereby to make sense of its infinite manifold. . . . The practice of social science is becoming aware that theory is its precondition.[4]

And indeed, as we are reminded by Herbert Blumer,

> [t]he possession and use of a prior picture or scheme of the empirical world under study . . . is an unavoidable prerequisite for any study of the empirical world. *One can see the empirical world only through some scheme or image of it.* The entire act of scientific study is oriented and shaped by the underlying picture of the empirical world that is used. This picture sets the selection and formulation of problems, the determination of what are data, the means to be used in getting data, the kinds of relations sought between data, and the forms in which propositions are cast.[5]

As for myself, I have never been attracted to the data-driven, fact-gathering approach to conducting research.[6] At the same time, however, nor have I ever bought the conventional premise that

I should therefore necessarily be testing existing theories. Defying such seemingly binary choice between inductive ("bottom-up") empiricism and deductive ("top-down") positivism,[7] I have thus developed over the past four and a half decades yet another approach to conducting sociological research that is *theoretically yet not necessarily "Theory"-driven*, which I actually characterize as *concept-driven*.[8]

Concept-driven research defies the seemingly binary conventional distinction between the acts of "describing" and "explaining," instead highlighting the acts of identifying *patterns* and *analyzing* them. When conducting such research, one's goal is indeed identifying and analyzing socially patterned phenomena in an attempt to reveal their fundamental features. I therefore refer to such intellectual endeavor as *social pattern analysis*.[9]

*Concepts*, of course, constitute the metaphorical lenses through which concept-driven researchers access the empirical world,[10] their role being defined primarily in terms of *attentional sensitization*. Essentially sensitizing researchers' attention,[11] they thus help give them a general sense of what they might find relevant to attend to by effectively suggesting to them "where" to look, like the mental templates that help birders and mushroomers notice a particular kind of bird or mushroom. In the words of one mushroomer, "*[i]t's not an eyesight; it's a mindset. If you just walk around with your head down, I swear you won't see anything. . . . There is always a little template that you carry in your mind.*"[12] Essentially resting "on a general sense of what is relevant," *sensitizing concepts*, as Blumer so aptly dubbed them, thus provide researchers with "a general sense of reference and guidance in approaching empirical instances. . . . [They] suggest directions along which to look."[13] Like magnets attached to their minds, they figuratively "attract" empirical data to their awareness, thereby helping them collect many they would have probably overlooked otherwise.[14]

Over the past four and a half decades I have indeed managed to bring into academic attention many socially patterned phenomena that had prior to that escaped it due to certain traditional conventions of sociological relevance.[15] As Marcel Proust bluntly put it, "[t]he only true voyage of discovery" may actually be "not to visit strange lands but to possess other eyes,"[16] and like eating the fruits of the proverbial tree of knowledge (that is, awareness) for Adam and Eve, it is the figurative *eye-opening*[17] function of the sensitizing concepts I have been using that has indeed allowed me to mentally access those hitherto "invisible" phenomena. "[A] new perspective opens up, *allowing things formerly not perceived to come into view. This* permits a new and previously inaccessible way of thinking about something."[18]

Such *mental magnets* were very helpful, for example, when I was writing *The Fine Line: Making Distinctions in Everyday Life*, which I was actually thinking about as my "boundaries book." By using the concept "boundary," I thus developed a heightened sensitivity to the various mental distinctions we make every day, such as between "warm" and "cold," "young" and "old," "fiction" and "nonfiction," or "crime" and "misdemeanor." Having essentially "primed" myself to notice boundary-like phenomena, I in fact generated between the time I started thinking about writing the book and the time I completed it ten years later hundreds of distinctions-related observations. And the meager number of such observations I have actually generated in comparison since then—a thirty-year period throughout which my "boundary" magnet has effectively been figuratively deactivated—only further attests to the formidable role of attentional sensitization in concept-driven research.

In the initial stages of a project, the object of the researcher's attention is often still defined in terms of vaguely formulated, hazy mental constructs respectively characterized by Ludwik Fleck and Robert Merton as mere *proto-ideas*[19] or *proto-concepts*.[20] Far from being fully formed, such "pre-ideas"[21] are often inarticulable, yet even at that early stage they already guide the researchers' attention in terms of "where" to look for social patterns. Once they actually begin to collect their data, however, such early pre-ideas gradually become mentally crisper as the initial *sensitizing proto-concepts* become increasingly sharper and thus more explicitly articulable.

While all researchers face the fundamental epistemic dilemma of what they should attend to and what they can effectively ignore, concept-driven researchers are particularly conscious of the *selective* manner in which they attend to the social world, essentially confining their attention to only a few selected aspects of the communities, organizations, or events they study.[22] After all, even if their project happens to be situated *in* a specific organization, it is by no means necessarily a study *of* that organization.[23] Although my doctoral dissertation study, for example, "took place *in* a hospital, it was never intended as a study *of* the hospital":[24]

> I knew before I entered the hospital that my intention would not be to produce an exhaustive ethnography of hospital life, but, rather, to isolate its temporal aspects only. . . . If I presumed to innovate in any way, it was certainly not in my selection of the setting to be observed, but, rather, in my choice of the analytical perspective from which to observe it. . . . I [thus] focused my observations on *only one aspect of hospital life, namely, its temporal structure*, deliberately ignoring . . . the history of the hospital, its national reputation, the quality of its patient care, its architectural design and spatial organization, its finances, the religious and ethnic makeup of its staff, and so on.[25]

Attending to the community, organization, or event one studies selectively presupposes, of course, the mental act of *focusing*.[26] After all, even in the "hard" sciences, "[t]he operations and measurements that a scientist undertakes in the laboratory . . . are not what the scientist sees—at least *not before . . . his attention [is] focused*."[27]

The process of focusing basically involves discerning figure-like "signals" from the background-like (and therefore effectively irrelevant) "noise" within which they are perceptually or conceptually embedded,[28] as when looking for a particular brand of shampoo in the supermarket: "[Y]ou would actually 'set' your attention . . . to *screen out* bottles that look different from [that] brand. . . . You'd let your eyes scan the shelf, paying little attention to most of the shampoo, *zeroing in* quickly on the one you wanted."[29] The effectively irrelevant bottles are thus

> passed over so quickly that they seem blurred. In a sense they are not seen at all. In much the same way one sees, but does not see, dozens of hurrying figures when trying to locate a friend in a busy air terminal.[30]

Given concept-driven researchers' fundamentally theoretical orientation, it is particular theoretical concerns that guide their attention in their search for "theoretically relevant"[31] data. And indeed, in sharp contrast to the effectively data-driven "grounded theory" approach,[32] for example, which at least initially proceeds from the empirical to the theoretical, *concept-driven sociology*[33] proceeds from the theoretical to the empirical. Unlike grounded-theory practitioners, concept-driven sociologists actually establish their initial theoretical concerns before they even start collecting their data. It is their unmistakably conceptual *focus*, indeed, that drives the empirical part of their research.[34]

In short, concept-driven sociologists start collecting their data only after having committed themselves to a particular conceptual *topic*. After all, as we are reminded by Howard Schwartz and Jerry Jacobs, they "are in the business of *studying sociological topics, not people*. . . . Their job is to make a set of integrated observations on a given topic and place them in an *analytical* framework."[35] As such, they study whiteness rather than whites, liberalism rather than liberals, and poverty rather than the poor. Establishing such *focal commitment* thus constitutes the very first step in their research.

Choosing that topic, as I keep reminding my students, is in fact the most critically consequential part of any concept-driven research project, as it provides researchers with a general sense of attentional "direction,"[36] thereby helping them notice social patterns which might have never emerged in mere perception.[37] I could never have collected the kind of data I did, for example, in my books *Taken for Granted, The Fine Line, The Elephant in the Room, Time Maps,* and *Ancestors and Relatives* had I not first committed myself to respectively focusing on default assumptions, distinctions, conspiracies of silence, historical narratives, and visions of genealogical relatedness as the unmistakably conceptual topics of my research.

## The Focused Mind

While the general methodological approach presented here is certainly not a logico-deductive one, nor, for that matter, is it strictly empirico-inductive. John Locke notwithstanding, the researcher's mind is not a tabula rasa, and even what may seem like a "chance" observation can indeed "enter" it only if s/he is mentally "prepared" for it.[38] As Louis Pasteur famously put it, "[i]n the fields of observation chance favors only the mind which is prepared."[39] It is their *epistemic readiness,* in other words, "the mind prepared to utilize scientific imagination," that allows researchers to "grasp the opportunity offered by 'chance' observation."[40]

Consider, for example, in this regard the discovery of the asteroids in the early nineteenth century. Strictly perceptually, after all, given the state of eighteenth-century telescopy, at least the larger ones could have certainly been spotted much earlier, yet it was actually only the discovery of Uranus in the 1780s, the first "new" planet to be discovered in several millennia, that epistemically prepared an entire generation of astronomers to the possibility of perhaps spotting yet additional ones.[41] Only their new attentional sensitivity to such a possibility, indeed, can account for the not-so-coincidental discovery of the three largest asteroids by two different astronomers between 1801 and 1807.[42]

By the same token, although the socially naive question, "Daddy, what's Thursday?" posed to me by my three-year-old daughter was the actual spark that inspired me to write *The Seven-Day Circle*, my study of artificial social rhythms that are longer than the solar day and shorter than the lunar month,[43] I might never have even given it a second thought had I not been epistemically prepared prior to that by having read Peter Berger and Thomas Luckmann's *The Social Construction of Reality*[44] not to take culturally reified social conventions such as the seven-day week for granted.[45] In a similar vein, although watching double-bassist Edgar Meyer play the habitually inattended bass line of a Bach Brandenburg Concerto actually sparked my decision to write *Hidden in Plain Sight*, my study of inattention,[46] I might not have even noticed him playing it had I not been epistemically prepared prior to that by having read Harold Garfinkel's *Studies in Ethnomethodology*[47] to think sociologically about "background"-like phenomena we habitually take for granted and thereby inattend.[48]

Similarly, when I was collecting the data for my book *Patterns of Time in Hospital Life*, it was my prior interest in the moral aspect of punctuality that led me to note the way doctors and nurses responded to latecomers,[49] and my prior interest in the temporal delineation of professional responsibility that sensitized me to otherwise-trivial events such as calling an off-duty nurse at home.[50] I would have most likely also failed to notice in which kinds of situations hospital staff would refer to their own watches and in which ones to the hospital wall clocks had I not been already theoretically sensitized to the specific functions of different timepieces.[51]

Equally revealing in this regard was my heightened attentional sensitivity to doctors' and nurses' responses to situations that deviated from the hospital's typically regular and therefore socially expected temporal order. Consider, for example, the case of a unit whose attending physician would always arrive at 10:00 for his daily conference with his medical team following their routine morning round, which was usually completed around 9:30. One morning the round was still not over a few minutes past 10:00 when the resident and the intern suddenly saw the attending arriving at the unit. Both of them immediately glanced at their watches, obviously trying to "make sense" of the cognitively incongruous coincidence of their morning round and the attending's arrival, which rarely coincided.[52] I would have probably never even noticed their response had I not been already attentionally sensitized to it by the concept "temporal regularity."[53]

Indeed, as the obvious product of attentional sensitization, *epistemic preparedness* usually implies the use of sensitizing concepts. Thus, it was my admittedly still-vague proto-conceptual notion of "the social organization of time,"[54] for example, that nevertheless guided my decision what to consider relevant to my study and therefore attend to, thereby sensitizing me to dozens of time-related social patterns I would have probably missed without it. By the same token, it was the concept "temporal coordination"[55] that sensitized me to the way doctors and nurses organized their lunch breaks, days off, and vacations. And I would have probably never paid attention to hospital staff's actual time-measurement and time-reckoning vocabularies (and thereby also never given a second thought to disputes between nurses and patients over whether "There are three persons ahead of you" was an appropriate answer to the question "When will the doctor see me?")[56] had I not been already proto-conceptually sensitized to what I would later come to explicitly refer to as "temporal reference frameworks."[57]

Such epistemic dynamic operates even when the data one collects are only figuratively "observable." Thus, when writing *The Elephant in the Room*, for example, I found the concept "open secret" particularly helpful in heightening my attentional sensitivity to the social phenomenon commonly known as a "conspiracy of silence." I likewise found "the background" an extremely useful sensitizing concept when I was exploring in *Hidden in Plain Sight* what we habitually disregard as "irrelevant," which was also true of the concepts "continuity" and "discontinuity" when I examined in *Time Maps* the social construction of historical narratives,[58] as well as of the "bloodline" and "side branch" metaphors when I was analyzing social visions of genealogical and quasi-genealogical "relatedness" in *Ancestors and Relatives*.[59]

In fact, such epistemic dynamic also operates even when what one actually collects is the *absence* of certain data! Thus, for example, when I was writing *Taken for Granted*, using the linguistic concepts "marked" and "unmarked" helped sensitize me to our typically implicit conventional notions of ordinariness and normality, which we habitually take for granted and thereby assume by default. That explains my heightened attentional sensitivity to our tacit *non*-use of culturally redundant and therefore semiotically superfluous terms such as *working dad, female nurse,* and *openly straight*, in sharp contrast to our common use of their pronouncedly "marked" counterparts *working mom, male nurse,* and *openly gay*.[60] It also explains my heightened sensitivity to the pointedly added qualifiers in "*marital* rape," "*reverse* discrimination," and "*white-collar* crime,"[61] as well as to the way we conventionally distinguish "alternative" medical practices from those we consider simply "medicine."[62]

Furthermore, sensitizing concepts are in fact very helpful even in strictly theoretical projects that involve no actual data. Thus, for example, when trying in *Social Mindscapes* to call attention to the suprapersonal dimension of the way we think in an effort to lay the foundations for cognitive sociology,[63] it was Durkheim's notion of the "impersonal" aspect of human cognition[64] as well as Fleck's notion of "thought communities"[65] that sensitized me to our unmistakably social norms and traditions of perceiving, attending, classifying, and remembering.[66] At the same time, however, it was Pitirim Sorokin's notion of the "sociocultural" sensibility separating the social from the natural sciences[67] that heightened my attentional sensitivity to cognitive conventions that, while clearly suprapersonal, are nevertheless by no means universal.[68] Those three concepts, along with Alfred Schutz's notion of "intersubjectivity,"[69] thus played a critical role in heightening my sensitivity to the way we think not only as individuals and as human beings but also as social beings.

## Attentional Socialization

The concept-driven way of conducting research is significantly different from the way sociologists are conventionally trained to approach their objects of study in that it requires them to commit to a particular conceptual focus rather than to a particular statistical sampling procedure (as in survey research) or "field" (as in ethnographic research) and thereby stay rigorously "focused." In cultivating a *focused mind*,[70] so to speak, concept-driven sociologists thus resemble pearl divers,[71] birders, deminers, and security baggage screeners, all of whom basically try to "spot" figure-like "targets" by mentally detaching them from their background-like surroundings.[72]

Only by undergoing a process of professional *attentional socialization*[73] and thereby acquiring a "sociological imagination,"[74] indeed, do sociologists develop the distinctly sociological concept-centered attentional sensitivities that enable them to envision "social movements," "labor markets," "power structures," and "social support networks." Like the expert *attentional mentors*[75] who instruct students in special "appreciation" courses what to attend to when looking at a painting, listening to a piece of music, watching a film, or tasting a glass of wine, I therefore list on my graduate course syllabi not only the readings for each week but also the particular concepts on which I want students to focus while reading them. The list of readings for the "Classical Theory" class in which we begin to discuss the work of Georg Simmel, for example, is thus preceded by the following list of *focalizing concepts*: "social interaction," "forms of sociation," "social circles" and "social networks," "multiple affiliations," "divided and undivided commitment," "social mobility," and "social marginality"; while the list of readings for my "Cognitive Sociology" class on the social organization of attention is preceded by a similar list: "the social organization of relevance and noteworthiness," "attentional communities," "attentional traditions," "norms of attending and disattending," "attentional socialization," "attentional deviance," "attentional battles," "joint attention," "joint disattention," "agenda-setting," and "foregrounding." Perhaps not surprisingly, therefore, many of my students indeed later launch concept-driven research projects whose pronouncedly conceptual or proto-conceptual foci range from "intercultural interpretation,"[76] "intellectual snobbery,"[77] "dual organization,"[78] "the social construction of kinship,"[79] "the standardization of beauty,"[80] "integrated and segmented identities,"[81] "the politics of ambiguity,"[82] "the social construction of parity,"[83] "liminality,"[84] "sociomental connectedness,"[85] "marked and unmarked identities,"[86] and "contrast sets"[87] to "sociocognitive myopia and hyperopia,"[88] "abstinence-based identities,"[89] "sick-identity careers,"[90] "hyphenated identities,"[91] "sexpectations,"[92] "cognitive awakenings,"[93] "backhanded compliments,"[94] "mnemonic engineering,"[95] "temporary selfhood,"[96] "the semiotics of deservingness,"[97] " 'doing' identity,"[98] and "the politics of access and restriction."[99]

Practicing concept-driven sociology requires certain cognitive skills that I believe anyone can cultivate. Those particular skills (focusing, of course, as well as generalizing, "exampling," and analogizing), in fact, have actually been tacitly utilized by many sociologists yet rarely systematically analyzed.

In other words, concept-driven sociology presupposes an implicit methodology that, although thus far never fully articulated, can in fact be taught. My main goal here, therefore, is to make the mental processes underlying the practicing of such a sociology more explicit. That, indeed, is what this book is about.

# 2

# Generalizing

The sociologist is concerned with *King* John, not with
King *John*.
— Lewis A. Coser, *Masters of Sociological Thought*, 180

## A Generic Sociology

One of our most formidable cognitive skills is the ability to *generalize*, most spectacularly evident when we engage in *theorizing*.
Indeed, one of the most distinctive characteristics of a "theoretical"
statement is its *generalizability*. A "theory," in other words, usually
involves an attempt to apply it to more than just a specific situation (thereby implying an effort to establish what it is a particular
"case" of),[1] thus allowing people to transcend the specifics of the
particular study on which it is based and appreciate its nonspecific,
*general* implications.[2]

Social theorizing usually involves viewing specific objects (the
Chilean flag), situations (a particular co-sponsored symposium),
and events (the U.S. 2020 presidential race) as *exemplifying* certain general social phenomena (national symbols, collaboration,
competition) thereby *transcending their singularity*. Durkheim's
*The Elementary Forms of Religious Life*,[3] for instance, can thus be
read as a discussion of not only Australian Aboriginal totemism but
also religious systems *in general*. Max Weber's *The Protestant Ethic
and the Spirit of Capitalism*[4] can likewise be considered a statement about not just the specific relation between Protestantism and

*Generally Speaking*. Eviatar Zerubavel, Oxford University Press (2021). © Oxford University Press.
DOI: 10.1093/oso/9780197519271.001.0001.

capitalism but also the relations between cultural and economic systems *in general*.

Furthermore, as exemplified by works such as George Herbert Mead's *Mind, Self, and Society*, Talcott Parsons's *The Social System*, or Berger and Luckmann's *The Social Construction of Reality*,[5] there are also ample instances of sociological theorizing that are not specifically situated culturally, historically, or in any particular setting. Nobody, however, has promoted the vision of such pronouncedly *nonspecific* (and thereby decidedly *generic*) sociology more compellingly than Simmel.

Though also well known for his historically situated classic works on urbanism, money, and modernity, it was nevertheless Simmel's effort to introduce a pronouncedly "formal" vision of social life, which involves viewing the fundamental "forms" of sociation (domination, submission, conflict, intimacy, secrecy, exchange) as "independent of their specific instantiations" and thereby effectively "divorced from any particular place or time,"[6] that best captures his distinctive sociological legacy. In fact, as he explicitly proclaims in the opening chapter of his magnum opus, *Soziologie*, "There remains for a sociology in the strictest sense . . . nothing but the treatment of [such] forms."[7]

In its effort to transcend specificity, Simmel's *formal sociology*[8] thus resembles arithmetic, which basically deals with the relations between essentially generic quantities (so that two plus three, for example, thus equals five regardless of whether one is actually counting peaches, camels, or coats). It likewise resembles geometry, which basically deals with the strictly formal properties of physical objects[9] (so that the shape of a sphere, for instance, is effectively independent of whether it is made of paper, aluminum, or glass).

In *formal theorizing*[10] sociologists thus focus their attention on the generic rather than the specific, thereby transcending singular occurrences. Instead of studying specific groups, situations, or events, for instance, they therefore study essentially genericized *types* of groups, situations, and events.

In short, formal theorizing presupposes a pronouncedly generic outlook on social life distinctly characterized by its conscious disregard for specificity. And indeed, inspired by Blumer,[11] Robert Prus thus proposes an explicitly *generic sociology*[12] that would stand in sharp contrast to conventional studies of specific situations that, as such, are "inadequately cast to serve as clear instances of generic sociological categories."[13] Such a sociology, as one might expect, would help us "extract greater theoretical value" from the various studies we read, for example, "by overcoming the tendency to see each study as dealing with a specific group and setting, rather than a more general process."[14]

Indeed, *genericizing* social groups, situations, and events actually helps reveal social patterns that are effectively invisible to anyone interested only in the specific.[15] As we are reminded by Kai Erikson, while someone "walking down a busy sidewalk in New York City at rush hour" might find it "difficult to sense any pattern . . . in that scene," for someone standing on the fourteenth floor of a building looking down on that same scene

> [t]he streams of people moving along the sidewalk appear to be *patterned*. . . . [T]he view from the fourteenth floor [thus] suggests that there are commonalities in the midst of all those particularities that give social life its distinctive design. . . . *Those patterns [are in fact] the subject matters of sociology.*[16]

That, indeed, is why I refer to the epistemic endeavor to figuratively "distill" such generic patterns from the specific cultural, historical, and situational contexts in which concept-driven sociologists actually encounter them as "social pattern analysis."

Climbing to Erikson's metaphorical fourteenth floor, of course, presupposes the mental act of *abstraction*.[17] It is their ability to abstract, after all, that allows researchers to transcend the specific and identify generic patterns that "would never have emerged in mere perception."[18] Indeed, "[t]he more abstract one's way of conceiving things," the more likely one is to transcend singularity and "make generic discoveries."[19] As Simmel bluntly put it, "abstractions alone produce science out of . . . reality."[20]

Abstraction, however, presupposes *conceptualization*, since abstract patterns are "factored out of . . . reality," after all, "by means of . . . concept[s]."[21] "[A]bstraction . . . from this world of particulars, and the holding on to it, is possible only through conceptualization and necessitates, ultimately, a concept. That is to say, the very act of abstraction is an act of conception."[22]

As we are reminded by Blumer, this is particularly evident in science. "To speak of science without concepts," after all, is like speaking of "a carver without tools, a railroad without tracks, a mammal without bones, a love story without love."[23] Indeed, in pre-Galilean physics, for example, motion used to be

> identified with particular objects. No one conceived of it as distinct from . . . these particular concrete objects. It remained for Galileo . . . to make the *abstraction*. In his famous experiments in measuring the swing of the lamp in the Cathedral of Pisa, in dropping pellets from the leaning tower of Pisa, and in rolling balls down smooth inclined planes, Galileo was making a definite *shift from particular objects to general motion*. The swing of the lamp, the fall of the pellets, and the roll of the balls were separate happenings; a distinctive kind of movement inhered in each. Through *conception* Galileo abstracted a content . . . which in being identified by a term became a concept. By *conceptualization*, then, the item of motion became detached and held.[24]

Which brings us back to concept-driven sociology.

## Transcontextual Research

As one might expect given its pronounced quest for generalizability, generic sociology is fundamentally *transcultural* in its scope,[25] as evidenced in its distinctly *non-culture-bound* vocabulary. In sharp contrast to most ethnographic research, for example, its concerns transcend any specific cultural context. "Not fashion in Italian dress . . . but the *general* form of fashion," indeed, "is what interests Simmel."[26]

Our common tendency to mistake generality for universality[27] notwithstanding, however, that does not mean that non-culture-bound social patterns are therefore universal. As exemplified by purely conventional (rather than physically or biologically based) patterns such as organizing one's activities in accordance with a seven-day rhythm or tracing one's descent strictly patrilineally, "transcultural" does not necessarily imply "universal."

Generic sociology is also pronouncedly *transhistorical*,[28] as it involves a conscious effort to dissociate the particular situations one studies from their historically specific settings.[29] As Lewis Coser characterizes the fundamental contrast between the generic sociologist and the historian, who typically deals with the historically singular,

> particular historical events are unique: the murder of Caesar, the accession of Henry VIII, and the defeat of Napoleon at Waterloo are all events located at a particular moment in time and having a nonrecurrent significance. Yet, if one looks at history through the peculiar lenses of the sociologist, one need not concern himself with the uniqueness of these events but, rather, with their underlying uniformities.[30]

"The sociologist," as he so poignantly reminds us, "is concerned with *King* John, not with King *John*."[31]

Thus, for example, as Erikson points out in his book *Wayward Puritans*, so aptly subtitled *A Study in the Sociology of Deviance*,

> the following study should be viewed as *sociological rather than historical*. The data presented here have not been gathered in order to throw new light on the Puritan community in New England but to add something to our understanding of deviant behavior *in general*. . . . [T]he Puritan experience in America has been treated in these pages as an example of human life everywhere.[32]

As such, "it helps explain the behavior of other peoples *at other moments in time*, and not just the particular subjects of this study."[33]

Furthermore, generic sociology is also fundamentally *transsituational*,[34] as its concerns transcend the specific situations in which its data are actually collected. It is sometimes even *"transdomain,"* as those concerns often cut across supposedly separate "domains" of social life (business, politics, religion).[35]

Finally, like Euclidean geometry, generic sociology also involves a conscious *disregard of scale* (and, as such, is fundamentally *translevel*), as manifested in the researcher's epistemic readiness to purposely ignore the conventional distinction between "micro-," "meso-," and "macro-sociological" scholarship. Indeed, points out Barney Glaser, it "takes on its fullest generality when one realizes its power applied to *social structural units of any size*, large or small."[36] After all, as so brilliantly demonstrated by Simmel, all social "triads" share certain common formal features (such as the possibility of forming coalitions, for instance) regardless of whether they are made up of three individuals, companies, or entire countries.

In transcending the various specific contexts in which its data are actually situated, generic sociology thus implies the idea of *decontextualizing* them, thereby effectively promoting a fundamentally *transcontextual*[37] view of social life. Its essence, writes Simmel, is "the detachment of the pure fact of sociation, in all its manifold forms, from its connection with the most diverse contents."[38] Indeed, he adds, to mentally detach the generic forms of sociation from their specific contents is "the basis for the only, as well as the entire, possibility of a special science of society as such."[39]

## Theorizing Generically

The indisputable founder of generic sociology,[40] Simmel has by no means remained its sole practitioner. His pronounced penchant for viewing specific situations as but particular instantiations of generic patterns clearly also inspired the work of his "grandstudent" Everett Hughes[41] as well as of Hughes's own student Erving Goffman.[42] And having myself studied with Goffman, I too feel a strong pull toward following in my "great-great-grandmentor's"[43] theoretico-methodological footsteps and figuratively "distill" generic social patterns from the specific contexts in which I actually encounter them.

My first extensive experiment with transcontextuality was *The Fine Line*, where I used the same generic conceptual framework to theorize the mental partitions we envision separating adjoining yet socially distinct "neighborhoods," temporally contiguous yet culturally distinct "stages" in the life course, "masculinity" from "femininity," "whites" from "people of color," as well as who we can sleep with from who we consider sexually off-limits.[44] Yet I fully committed myself to an explicitly generic-sociological theoretico-methodological agenda only in *Time Maps*, where, in an effort to develop a strictly transcontextual approach to the way we collectively narrate our past, I consciously detached my data from the culturally, historically, domain-, and level-specific contexts in which I actually encountered them. Whether a particular national calendar I used there in my analysis was Libya's or Angola's, for instance,[45] was therefore only peripheral to my general interest in the strictly formal features of "calendrical commemoration" it helped reveal. I was likewise much less concerned with whether a particular envisioned "line" of monarchs I examined happened to be Persian, Ethiopian, or Bulgarian[46] than with the formal features of dynasties *in general* it helped highlight. As I pointed out in the introduction,

> my pronouncedly generic theoretical concerns call for an explicit commitment to *decontextualize* my findings by pulling them out of the culturally and historically specific environments within which I first happen to identify them, since my ultimate goal is to develop a *transcultural* as well as a *transhistorical* perspective on social memory as a generic phenomenon.[47]

By the same token, in *The Elephant in the Room*, rather than highlight the respective singularity of situations where people jointly avoid discussing a specific "uncomfortable" topic such as race,[48] homosexuality,[49] the threat of nuclear annihilation,[50] or the Holocaust,[51] I tried to focus strictly on their formal properties, thereby presenting such situations as but particular instances of a generic phenomenon, namely a "conspiracy" of silence. And most recently, in *Taken for Granted*, I likewise tried to transcend the specificity of our conventional habitual tendencies to take maleness, whiteness, straightness, or able-bodiedness for granted, effectively presenting them as but specific manifestations of our general tendency to assume "unmarkedness" by default.

As products of concept-driven projects, these as well as most of my other books exemplify Simmel's observation that sociology is ultimately "founded upon an abstraction from concrete reality."[52] And my epistemic commitment to transcontextuality is indeed quite evident even from just glancing at their subject indexes, which feature mostly abstract and thereby pronouncedly decontextualized conceptual entries such as "ambiguity," "compartmentalization," "polarization," and "insularity" (in *The Fine Line*),[53] "anachronism," "commemoration," "multilinearity," and "mnemonic socialization" (in *Time Maps*),[54] "open secrets," "co-denial," "enabling," and "undiscussables" (in *The Elephant in the Room*),[55] or "absence," "implicitness," "ordinariness," and "semiotic subversion" (in *Taken for Granted*),[56] rather than ones invoking a specific person, place, or event.

The pronouncedly transcontextual theoretico-methodological thrust of my work is further exemplified by my conscious effort to organize my books *thematically*, with each chapter effectively revolving around an unmistakably generic "theme"[57] that manifests itself *in various different contexts*. Thus, rather than organize *Time Maps* in chapters respectively featuring the specific ways in which collective memory manifests itself in the contexts of the family, the religious community, and the nation, for instance, I did it in ones respectively featuring pronouncedly generic topics such as the socio-mnemonic organization of historical continuity and the social construction of historical "beginnings," in each of which I actually discuss various such contexts.[58] By the same token, instead of organizing *Taken for Granted* in chapters respectively showcasing the ways in which the politico-semiotic act of "othering" manifests itself in the specific domains of race, gender, and sexuality, I thus broke it down into ones respectively featuring unmistakably generic transcontextual "themes" such as semiotic asymmetry, semiotic subversion, and the politics of normality, in each of which I actually discuss several such domains.[59]

In a similar vein, instead of organizing *The Elephant in the Room* in chapters respectively featuring specific contexts of conspiracies of silence such as those involving excessive drinking, organizational corruption, and domestic violence, I thus did it in unmistakably "thematic" ones respectively revolving around the formal structure of such "conspiracies," the politics of collective denial, and the dynamics of silence breaking, in each of which I actually discuss various such contexts.[60] And rather than organize *Ancestors and Relatives* in chapters respectively featuring each of the various levels of group "belongingness" in which genealogical identity manifests itself (the family, the ethnic community, the species), I thus did it in pronouncedly "thematic" ones respectively revolving around the tension between nature and culture, the politics of descent, and the "genealogical engineering" of the future, in each of which I actually address several of those levels.[61]

Many sociologists today tend to focus much of their attention on the specific, often at the expense of also exploring the generic. This book is an attempt to correct this unfortunate imbalance by examining the very theoretico-methodological process by which we can mentally "distill" generic social patterns from the culturally, historically, and situationally specific empirical contexts in which we actually happen to encounter them.

Having introduced the fundamental logic underlying the process of *generic theorizing*, I turn now to examine the actual "mechanics" of conducting transcontextual research.[62] It is therefore time now to present the two other major theoretico-methodological tactics (that is, other than focusing and generalizing) that are particularly helpful in this process, namely "exampling" and analogizing.

# 3

# Exampling

> Whereas the classic ethnographer seeks thick description
> and thin but widely spread analysis of a specific social set-
> ting so that it is understood in all its contours and details,
> the cognitive sociologist prefers *thick analysis and thin but*
> *widely spread description* of social settings that reveal the
> analytic principles being studied.
>
> —Wayne Brekhus, "The Rutgers School," 458.
>
> Emphasis added

We have yet to establish what actually constitutes "data" in concept-
driven research. And in order to do that, we need to examine the
theoretico-methodological practice of *exampling*.

There are two fundamentally contrasting modes of theorizing
effectively associated with two contrasting brands of scholars,
observes Avishai Margalit, namely "*e.g.* philosophers and *i.e.*
philosophers—illustrators and explicators. Illustrators trust, first
and foremost, striking examples, in contrast with explicators, who
trust, first and foremost, definitions and general principles."[1] "I see
merit in both styles," he adds, "but by temperament if not by con-
viction I subscribe to *e.g.* philosophy."[2]

Extrapolating this fundamental distinction between "i.e.-
style" and "*e.g.-style*" *theorizing* to sociology, so, indeed, do
I. Furthermore, I would even argue that in concept-driven sociological research *examples* often *are* the data, lying as they do at the
heart of the thus-far-undertheorized practice of exampling.

*Generally Speaking*. Eviatar Zerubavel, Oxford University Press (2021). © Oxford University Press.
DOI: 10.1093/oso/9780197519271.001.0001.

As any experienced teacher probably knows, exampling is an exceptionally effective pedagogical tool. Thus, when introducing a new concept in class, for instance, I find it particularly helpful to give students a few examples illustrating its potential applicability.

Furthermore, as demonstrated time and again by philosophers, economists, and linguists, *examples can also be extremely useful as actual data.* And indeed, in concept-driven sociology, data often come in the form of specific empirical ("real-life") *illustrations* of various generic social patterns of which they serve as "representative" instances or "cases."[3] Through the use of concrete "cases in point," the singularity of which they nevertheless consciously disregard, concept-driven researchers can thereby empirically "ground" their ideas by essentially *instantiating* those typically abstract and therefore initially difficult-to-grasp patterns.

## Contextual Diversity

Yet how do generic sociologists select the examples they use in their analyses? Indeed, given the obvious etymological affinity between "example" and "sample," how do they actually go about *sampling* the data they collect?

As one might expect, the very notion of generic theorizing precludes the idea of confining the collection of one's data to a single specific "case-study." Only a *multicase*[4] analysis of the "Republic of Texas," "Freemen of Montana," "Tupac Amaru," and "MOVE" standoffs as well as the ones at Ruby Ridge, Waco, and Wounded Knee, for example, could allow Robin Wagner-Pacifici to indeed theorize the "standoff" as a generic social phenomenon.[5] And only a multicase analysis of the O. J. Simpson, Mike Tyson, Central Park jogger, Bensonhurst, William Kennedy Smith, and Rodney King high-profile criminal cases could likewise allow Lynn Chancer to theorize the tendency to legally as well as journalistically sympathize with *either* one side *or* the other as a generic phenomenon, namely "partialization."[6]

A generic sociology, in short, calls for *multicontextual* data.[7] In order to be able to identify generic (and, as such, transcontextual) social patterns, in other words, one needs to encounter them in multiple social contexts, and the greater the number of contexts in which one collects one's data, of course, the more generalizable the patterns they help reveal. *Trans*contextuality therefore implies *multi*contextuality.

Yet generalizability is a function of not only the size but also the range of one's research sample, which implies the need to identify social patterns "across a *wide* range of social contexts."[8] One's ability to generalize, after all, "is not simply a function of the number of units one has observed. More important are the *kinds* of units observed, that is, the range of characteristics of the units investigated,"[9] and it is indeed the "range of characteristics included in a sample" that "increases the range of population characteristics to which generalization is possible."[10] In research as well as teaching, the effectiveness of the examples one uses thus largely depends on selecting ones that are significantly *different* from one another. After all, the more similar they are, the less effective the very practice of *multi-exampling*.

When I was writing my first book, *Patterns of Time in Hospital Life*, I viewed it as a generic-sociological study of the temporal organization of social life *in general*. As I disappointingly enough soon came to realize, however, since I had actually collected all my data in a hospital it was hard for people not to view it as a study of hospital life *specifically*. (Indeed, the first category the Library of Congress chose for cataloging it was "Hospitals—Sociological Aspects"!) By collecting all my data in a single specific context, in other words, I actually made it difficult for my readers to appreciate the potential applicability of my analysis to others. I promptly applied the lesson I learned from that methodological faux pas in my next book, *Hidden Rhythms*, where I consciously chose to situate my generic-sociological study of schedules and calendars in a *wide variety* of cultural and historical contexts (Orthodox Judaism, medieval Benedictine monasticism, the French Revolution) as well as substantive "domains" (work, politics, religion), thereby making it absolutely clear to my readers that the book was not about either of those but, rather, about time.[11]

Indeed, in order to be able to identify generic (and therefore transcontextual) social patterns, one needs to consider not just the sheer number but also the *diversity* of the contexts represented in one's research sample. That implies collecting one's data not only in a lot of contexts but also in a wide range of diverse ones.[12]

Generic sociology, in short, requires making a conscious commitment to draw in one's research on a *broad* base of data. "[R]ather than developing a thick and deep description of a narrow slice of social life," it thus calls for "an analytically deep analysis that covers *a wide empirical range* of social life."[13]

Indeed, as I describe the theoretico-methodological practice of exampling in both *Time Maps* and *The Elephant in the Room*,

> [s]uch pronouncedly generic concerns also call for a conscious effort to draw on a substantively *broad base* of concrete evidence. Ultimately interested in identifying formal mnemonic patterns that transcend any specific context of remembering, I thus illustrate my arguments with specific examples from *a particularly wide range* of such contexts. Instead of focally confining myself to one specific case study . . . I therefore draw my evidence from *a wide range* of cultural as well as historical contexts. I likewise examine *a wide variety* of specific domains (science, religion, politics). . . . Needless to say, the wider the range of the contexts on which I draw in my analysis, the broader its generalizability.[14]

In an effort to highlight general patterns that transcend any particular social situation, I therefore do not present any in-depth case study of a specific conspiracy of silence. I instead use numerous illustrative examples eclectically drawn from *a wide range of substantive contexts*. Indeed, the broader the substantive base of evidence on which I draw in my analysis, the greater the generalizability of the observations I can make about the structure and dynamics of collective denial. Throughout the book I therefore deliberately oscillate between *widely disparate contexts* in order to emphasize the distinctly generic properties of conspiracies of silence.[15]

In so doing, I thus follow in the methodological footsteps of master-exampler Goffman, who summed up this practice as follows: "I take *a large number of illustrations, variously obtained* . . . and try to get a formulation that is compatible with all of them."[16]

Given their quest for social patterns "spanning diverse settings" across *"widely different contexts,"*[17] generic sociologists indeed make a special effort to select for their research samples *"dissimilar substantive groups* . . . in order to increase [their] theory's scope."[18] Most spectacular, in this regard, are explicit efforts to effectively *maximize the diversity* of the contexts from which they actually gather their data. After all,

a finding emerging from the study of several very heterogeneous sites would be more robust and thus more likely to be useful in understanding various other sites than one emerging from the study of several very similar sites. Heterogeneity can be obtained by searching out sites that will provide *maximal variation*.[19]

In other words, *the wider the range of one's empirical data, the more generalizable one's theoretical claims.*

Arlie Hochschild's analysis of the social organization of human feelings[20] is a perfect case in point. In order to enhance the diversity of her research sample, Hochschild thus chose to interview members of two temperamentally *contrasting* occupations, namely flight attendants, who are professionally socialized to project pleasantness, and bill collectors, by contrast, who are specifically trained

to appear intimidating. Equally exemplary in this regard is Asia
Friedman's analysis of the way we attribute maleness or femaleness to human bodies we visually encounter.[21] In order to make her
analysis more generalizable, Friedman likewise chose to interview
members of two groups representing *contrasting* levels of expertise
in making such attributions, namely the *least* and the *most* profi-
cient users of visual information about sexed bodies: While "transgender people possess . . . 'expert knowledge' about seeing sex,"
"blind people made interesting informants primarily because they
do *not* participate in visual sex attribution."[22] In order to enhance
the diversity of the contexts where they collected their data, both
Hochschild and Friedman thus opted to draw on ones that are *max-
imally different* from each other.

My effort to maximize the *contextual diversity* of my data also
informs the way I read.[23] Valorizing breadth, I thus *eclectically*
sample, sometimes even in the very same reading session, various
diverse sources rather than habitually confining myself to a formu-
laically assembled as well as ritualistically co-cited narrow group
of texts conventionally canonized as "*the* literature." Substantively
speaking, of course, Oswald Spengler's *The Decline of the West*,
Richard Sorabji's *Time, Creation, and the Continuum*, Pitirim
Sorokin's *Social and Cultural Mobility*, George Simpson's *Principles
of Animal Taxonomy*, Barbara Herrnstein Smith's *Poetic Closure*,
Robert Sommer's *Personal Space*, Werner Sollors's *Beyond Ethnicity*,
Camillo Sitte's *The Art of Building Cities*, Robert Sokal's "Clustering
and Classification," Sally Springer and Georg Deutsch's *Left Brain,
Right Brain*, Peter Singer's *Animal Liberation*, and June Singer's
*Androgyny* have very little in common. Respectively written by a
historian, a philosopher, a sociologist, a paleontologist, a literary
critic, an environmental psychologist, a professor of African-
American studies, an architect, a biostatistician, a neuropsycholo-
gist, a bioethicist, and a Jungian analyst, they may have never been
read and thereby cited together before. Yet as pronouncedly diverse
readings that have therefore helped broaden the way I think about

boundaries and distinctions, they are indeed all listed on the very same page of the bibliography of *The Fine Line!*[24]

In *exampling multicontextually*, generic sociologists thus embrace contextual diversity, ready to sacrifice substantive coherence to ensure *focal coherence*. Such diversity, as we shall now see, may be manifested multi-culturally, multihistorically, multisituationally, as well as at multiple levels of social aggregation.

## Cultural and Historical Diversity

Given the decidedly transcultural scope of their concerns, generic sociologists may thus choose to conduct *multi-cultural* research.[25] As exemplified, for instance, by Simmel's discussion of English, Venetian, and Peruvian manifestations of "divide-and-rule" politics,[26] using data from *multiple, diverse cultural contexts* enhances the likelihood that the social patterns they help reveal are indeed generic. In order to be able to identify transcultural and thereby generic patterns of social remembrance,[27] for example, I had to collect my data from a wide range of cultural contexts rather than confine myself to a single culturally specific case study, a common tradition in collective-memory studies that has indeed yielded few attempts to generalize beyond specific societies. Only by drawing on the highly diverse cultural contexts of Mexico, Denmark, Tunisia, and Japan, for instance,[28] could I in fact produce a pronouncedly transcultural analysis of "calendrical commemoration" as a generic social phenomenon.

As one might expect, being able to identify transcultural and thereby generic social patterns almost inevitably implies the need to draw not only on one's own data but also on ones collected by others. As such, it also implies the need to overcome the professional timidity often associated with the prospect of being considered a "dilettante." Our conventional tendency to conflate being a specialist with being an "expert" (and therefore also being a *generalist*, by contrast, with being a "mere amateur") keeps many potential generic sociologists, I believe, from engaging in some kind of multi-cultural research.[29]

But generic theorizing involves collecting data from multiple social settings "widely scattered" in space as well as in time,[30] thereby raising the need for not only multi-cultural but also *multihistorical* research, in an effort to reveal not only transcultural but also transhistorical social patterns. As demonstrated, for instance, by Orlando Patterson, a formal theory of slavery thus calls for examining the practice of slaveholding in dozens of societies around the world *as well as throughout history*.[31] By the same token, as demonstrated by Raoul Naroll, a formal theory of military deterrence may likewise call for comparing the military situation in eighteenth-century England with those in eleventh-century China, fourteenth-century Switzerland, eighth-century Byzantium, seventeenth-century France, fifteenth-century Russia, as well as fourth-century Rome.[32]

Along similar lines, throughout *Time Maps*, I thus draw on data from not only multiple diverse cultural contexts but also a *wide range of historical periods*, as when I examine sixteenth-, seventeenth-, eighteenth-, twentieth-, and twenty-first-century instances of the politico-mnemonic practice of drawing "parallels" between past and current historical situations.[33] Drawing on extremely disparate historical contexts such as those of early Christianity and the French Revolution[34] has likewise been part of my conscious effort to develop a pronouncedly transhistorical perspective on the politics of time.[35]

To make the focal coherence of the seemingly unconnected examples one draws from such disparate historical contexts more apparent, it might also be useful to consciously juxtapose them when presenting them, thereby tacitly implying that they are but various historically specific instantiations of the very same generic social phenomenon. A perfect example in this regard is Simmel's classic culturally as well as historically multicontextual portrayal, in the very same paragraph, of the role of intergroup conflict in fostering intragroup cohesion:

> France owes the consciousness of its national unity only to its fight against the English, and only the Moorish war made the Spanish regions into one people. . . . The United States needed the War of Independence; Switzerland, the fight against Austria; the Netherlands, rebellion against Spain; the Achaean League, the struggle against Macedonia; and the founding of the new German Empire furnishes a parallel to all of these instances.[36]

By the same token, when discussing conspiracies of silence surrounding political atrocities in *The Elephant in the Room*, I likewise refer *in the very same sentence* to fellow Arab leaders' initial reluctance to publicly denounce Saddam Hussein's brutal invasion and occupation of Kuwait, fellow African leaders' persistent unwillingness to publicly condemn Robert Mugabe's abysmal civil-rights record in Zimbabwe, and Western intellectuals' equally prolonged refusal to publicly acknowledge the horrors of Stalinism.[37]

## Situational Diversity

Yet identifying generic and therefore transcontextual social patterns may also call for conducting *multisituational* research even within the same culture as well as historical period. "[F]ormal theory," after all, "cannot . . . work very well when written from only one substantive area."[38]

At a minimum, that might imply conducting *multisite* studies, as exemplified, for instance, by Calvin Morrill's study of patterns of executive conflict management in thirteen different corporations.[39] Yet it might also involve conducting those studies in multiple *kinds* of situations, let alone in *multiple social "domains"* that "are far apart,"[40] such as when comparing a hospital to a school rather than to other hospitals.[41]

Although *multidomain exampling* may also take place at the multi-project level, as exemplified by Gary Fine's four-decade study of small-group "idiocultures" in a dozen different social contexts ranging from chess playing, Little League baseball, fantasy role-playing games, and mushrooming to culinary training, weather forecasting, high-school debating, and political activism,[42] it is usually done within the same project. Thus, when theorizing the phenomenon of the "scandal," for instance, Ari Adut examines moral, political, as well as artistic controversies about sex, corruption, as well as aesthetic transgression.[43] By the same token, when introducing his study of "the public sphere," he points out that he draws his examples from a highly diverse,

> *wide array* of cases: homosexuality in Victorian England, the 2008 stock market crash, anti-Semitism in Europe, confidence in American presidents, electoral and congressional voting, communications in social media, the court of Louis XIV, special prosecutor investigations, the visibility of African Americans, the Reign of Terror during the French Revolution, the Islamic veil, sexual politics in America, public executions, and pricing in contemporary art.[44]

Multidomain exampling is further evidenced in Julius Roth's analysis of patients', soldiers', and prisoners' "career timetables"; Andrew Abbott's study of the process of professionalization among lawyers, librarians, and psychiatrists; Dan Ryan's observations about students', investors', and research subjects' respective rights to be notified about their course requirements, their company's financial situation, and the project in which they are asked to participate; as well as Paul McLean's discussion of the internet's role in the modern diffusion of rumors, religious ideas, fashion, and political protest.[45] It is likewise exemplified by my discussion, in

*The Fine Line*, of the multiple diverse manifestations of the "rigid-minded" manner of classifying reality (rules of endogamy, food taboos, specialized music radio stations),[46] as well as by my pronouncedly multisituational analysis of conspiracies of silence in *The Elephant in the Room*, where I refer almost interchangeably to the silences often surrounding domestic violence, homosexuality, and the Holocaust, let alone someone's stutter, bad breath, or open fly.[47]

Furthermore, following once again in Simmel's rhetorical footsteps, I thus also discuss there in the very same sentence the role of silence-breaking in fights against multiple (both political and sexual, for instance) forms of violence:

> [T]here are many social movements whose entire raison d'être is to raise public awareness of otherwise backgrounded social problems. The public demonstrations held by the Mothers of the Plaza de Mayo to protest Argentina's "Dirty War" against its political dissidents in the late 1970s were a classic example of such collective elephant-foregrounding, as are Take Back the Night rallies aimed at raising public awareness of sexual violence against women.[48]

By the same token, in *Taken for Granted*, I juxtapose in the same paragraph multiple, substantively diverse manifestations of the phenomenon of "semiotic asymmetry":

> The main purpose of marking is the establishment of a fundamental semiotic asymmetry between "marked" and "unmarked." Such asymmetry is manifested, for example, in the pronouncedly uneven semiotization of streets that are specifically marked with "Do Not Enter" signs and ones that are *not* marked with "Please Enter" ones, food products that are explicitly labeled "organic" and ones that have *no* labels specifically marking them as tainted by the use of pesticides, and explicitly marked bike lanes and ones

that are *not* specifically designated "car lanes." By the same token, in stark contrast to parking spots and public-restroom stalls specifically designed for people with disability, there are none specifically designed for the able-bodied. Like the term *openly straight*, the latter member of each of these nominally symmetrical semiotic pairs is assumed by default and therefore taken for granted. As such, unlike its nominally equivalent counterpart, it is effectively considered semiotically superfluous.[49]

My pursuit of transcontextuality also informs my teaching, as I urge students to use *multiple examples from diverse contexts* in an effort to identify generic social patterns. To ensure the generalizability of those patterns, I point out, they need to extrapolate from the specific contexts where they initially encounter them to multiple other contexts. Thus, for example, in my "Classical Theory" course, I specifically ask students to use key sociological concepts like "social fact" and "ideal type" in other contexts than the ones originally used by Durkheim and Weber when introducing them.

Indeed, multicontextual exampling is a distinctive trademark of many of my students' work.[50] A typical example is Kristen Purcell's pronouncedly multidomain analysis of the social effort to establish competitive parity, whether in antitrust laws, affirmative-action programs, sport, college admissions, or beauty pageants.[51] So, for that matter, is Jamie Mullaney's examination of the way abstinence operates "as a generic category of identity organization"[52] whether it involves abstaining from smoking, sex, meat, dairy products, television, alcohol, driving, illegal drugs, or having children.[53] And as he analyzes patterns of "personal discovery," Thomas DeGloma likewise draws on multiple instances of existential "awakening" (and thereby "seeing the light") almost interchangeably regardless of whether they are part of religious, political, or sexual "conversions."[54]

## Multilevel Research

*Theorizing transcontextually* may also involve *multilevel* research across the microsocial–macrosocial spectrum. Following Simmel's classic discussion of social triangularity,[55] for example, we can thus expect a formal analysis of "triadic" relations to include those between a father, a mother, and their daughter as well as those between Congress, the White House, and the Supreme Court and the ones between the United States, Russia, and the Ukraine. A formal theory of social exchange would likewise reveal the importance of reciprocity between friends, neighboring communities, as well as sovereign states.

Consider also in this regard my discussion of the critical role of social exclusion in helping delineate the perceived boundaries of families, professional groups, religious denominations, as well as entire nations:

> Social identity is always exclusionary, since any inclusion necessarily entails some element of exclusion as well. . . . In order for any group to be perceived as a separate entity, it must have some nonmembers who are excluded from it. . . . If membership in the French nation, the American Bar Association, the Presbyterian church, or the Vanderbilt family is to be meaningful, there must be at least some individuals who are explicitly excluded from such collectivities.[56]

By the same token, I also examine the way collective remembrance manifests itself at the levels of both families and world religions,[57] as well as the manner in which both small organizations and entire societies manage to "co-deny" the obvious presence of inconvenient "elephants" such as corruption and political incompetence in their midsts.[58] And I likewise discuss the multiple levels of social belongingness (the family, the nation, the species) at which the phenomenon of "genealogical identity" typically manifests itself,[59] thereby addressing the sense of "cousinhood" we may experience at the multiple levels of the way we are genealogically "related" to our first cousins, fellow nationals, as well as fellow human beings.

We have thus far examined three of the four theoretico-methodological pillars of concept-driven sociology, namely focusing, generalizing, and exampling. Let us turn now to examine its fourth pillar, namely analogizing.

# 4

# Analogizing

[T]he ways gay men organize their identity ought to also
reveal something about how Christians, Democrats,
feminists, doctors, bird watchers, mothers, African
Americans, Italians, southerners, Gen X'ers, baseball fans,
vegetarians, drug dealers, kindergarten teachers, and jazz
musicians organize their identities.

—Wayne Brekhus, *Peacocks, Chameleons,*
*Centaurs,* 137–38

## The Analogical Imagination

*Multi*contextual exampling also opens the door for *cross*-contextual
comparisons. Indeed, it implies "a conscious and explicit *compara-*
*tive* agenda that seeks to identify the conditions under which extant
theoretical concepts or perspectives on generic social processes
may be extended."[1] In other words, it promotes the use of "the
comparative method," explicitly identified by Auguste Comte, the
founder of modern sociology, as one of its foremost methodological tools.[2] It is one's epistemic commitment to thinking cross-
contextually (and thereby comparatively), indeed, that ensures the
*trans*contextual scope of one's work.

Yet sociology's vision of comparative research has traditionally
been modeled after Weber's classic studies of religious ethics, which
were actually designed to feature the distinctness of specific world
religions vis-à-vis one another (as by characterizing Protestantism,

*Generally Speaking.* Eviatar Zerubavel, Oxford University Press (2021). © Oxford University Press.
DOI: 10.1093/oso/9780197519271.001.0001.

for example, *in contrast to* Hinduism and Buddhism).[3] As such, comparative sociological analysis is specifically designed to highlight *variability*.

Given generic sociology's pronouncedly transcontextual agenda, however, the kind of comparative analysis it calls for is in fact designed to highlight the very opposite of substantive variability, namely formal *commonality*.[4] And while most comparativists indeed emphasize cross-contextual variability, generic sociologists actually use the act of comparing (that is, of "showing the likenesses between . . . things")[5] specifically in order to reveal *cross-contextual formal equivalence* despite substantive differences, thereby demonstrating "the usefulness of comparisons made . . . among the seemingly noncomparable,"[6] as when reminding those who say "How can you compare them? It's like comparing apples and oranges"[7] that both apples and oranges, after all, are fruits.

It is such quest for uncovering fundamental (formal) similarities between (substantively) different phenomena, indeed, that so distinctly characterizes generic sociology.[8] In sharp contrast to the conventional comparativist tendency to highlight differences between substantively distinct objects and occurrences, it regards the latter as but various manifestations of the very same transcontextual pattern.[9] My comparing a Romanian banknote featuring the country's last native ruler alongside the Roman emperor who conquered it to a Mexican monument featuring faces representing the country's Indian as well as Spanish roots is thus designed to highlight their formal equivalence as "parallel" instances of genealogical "braiding" (a form of narrating descent that acknowledges the multilinear character of a group's genealogical identity by preserving the memory of more than just one ancestral past)[10] rather than culturally specific distinctness.

One of the most distinctive characteristics of generic sociology, in other words, is the theoretico-methodological practice of "compar[ing] phenomena that may be radically different in concrete content"[11] in an effort to reveal formal equivalence across substantively disparate contexts and therefore also between substantively disparate phenomena.[12] And the more substantively diverse the contexts from which one picks one's examples, of course, the more striking the formal *parallels*[13] one reveals between them despite such diversity.

While making special efforts to diversify the contexts in which they collect their data, in short, generic sociologists thus nevertheless try to uncover similarities between seemingly disparate phenomena by *identifying common formal patterns across substantively diverse contexts.* Thus, when explaining her seemingly odd decision to study both flight attendants and bill collectors, for example, Hochschild indeed points out that "the *same* principles of emotional labor apply to very different jobs and very different feelings,"[14] thereby demonstrating the theoretico-methodological value of *noting fundamental equivalences despite substantive differences.* That is also true of the "seemingly disjointed" examples involving school shootings, child abductions, and "historically white" colleges invoked by Eduardo Bonilla-Silva in an effort to illustrate his pronouncedly transcontextual notion of "racial grammar."[15] By the same token, in *Time Maps*, I thus highlight the formal equivalence of ethnic garb, wedding anniversaries, and historic neighborhoods as substantively disparate yet nonetheless *analogous* symbolic "bridges" between the past and the present,[16] explicitly pointing out that while my commitment to multicontextual evidence calls for greater substantive diversity, my decision "to constantly oscillate between widely different contexts" is designed to highlight "their *common* rather than distinctive" features, since my goal is indeed "to identify the *common generic* underpinnings of the social structure of memory."[17]

"[T]he recognition that . . . different things can be treated as the same,"[18] or at least acknowledges certain "respects in which they are thought to be similar,"[19] presupposes *analogizing*, a mental process specifically designed to highlight *formal parallels across disparate contexts.* Indeed, "comparing similar events, activities, or phenomena despite variation"[20] is the distinctive hallmark of *thinking analogically*.

This is particularly critical for generic theorizing,[21] since it is the epistemic readiness to analogize, after all, that makes the transcendence of context (and therefore also singularity) possible. Indeed, the very practice of exampling, for instance, would be impossible without it.

One cannot emphasize enough the role of *analogies* in concept-driven sociology in general and generic sociology in particular. "[W]ithout analogies," after all, "there can be no concepts," since every concept, remind us Douglas Hofstadter and Emmanuel Sander, actually "owes its existence to a long succession of analogies made unconsciously over many years."[22] The very act of conceptualizing, or basically giving different things the same name,[23] indeed, implies a readiness to lump the various referents of a given concept together as being "similar" in some regard. Using a concept ("structure," "suggestion," "disease") thus presupposes one's epistemic readiness to disregard the differences among the various instantiations of the phenomenon it denotes and treat them as effectively "the same." In other words, it implies one's readiness to disregard context (and thus singularity).

No one, indeed, has promoted *analogical theorizing* more compellingly than the very founder of generic sociology. It is Simmel, after all, who insists that

> the same form of sociation can be observed in quite dissimilar contents . . . [T]he same form of interaction obtains among individuals in societal groups that are the most unlike imaginable in purpose and significance. Superiority, subordination, competition, division of labor, foundation of parties, representation, inner solidarity coupled with exclusiveness toward the outside, and innumerable similar features are found in the state as well as in a religious community, in a band of conspirators as in an economic association, in an art school as in a family.[24]

It is likewise Simmel who in fact invites sociologists to

> discover the laws of social forms only by collecting such societary
> phenomena of the most diverse contents, and by *ascertaining*
> *what is common to them in spite of their diversity*. In this way
> the diverse contents of the forms . . . nullify each other, and that
> which is formally the same, the societary form as such, must
> clearly appear.[25]

Urging comparativists to actually select their research cases "based
on *analogous circumstances* occurring in different social settings"[26]
(that is, to effectively "extract form from content" in an effort to uncover "common processes and structures in similar activities across
different social settings"),[27] Diane Vaughan indeed wittily dubs the
striking parallels among the substantively disparate instantiations
of formal social patterns "Simmelarities"![28]

Simmel's unmistakable, pronouncedly analogical style of social
theorizing also permeates the work of his grandstudent Hughes,
who, very much like him, also "displayed a genius for discerning
*similarities of pattern* among social phenomena of the most diverse sort,"[29] as exemplified by the strikingly parallel structural
situations of female and black professionals in 1940s America
as members of low-status social groups occupying high-status
professional positions.[30] It likewise permeates the work of his
great-grandstudent, master analogist Goffman, who consciously
disregards the obvious differences between boarding schools,
prisons, nursing homes, monasteries, and mental hospitals in an
attempt to uncover their formally equivalent (and therefore "parallel") socially insulating ("total") character,[31] as well as between
gay people, members of ethnic minorities, and persons with disability in an effort to highlight their "stigmatized" identities.[32]

Following in my great-great-grandmentor's, grandmentor's,
and mentor's theoretico-methodological footsteps, I too *consciously disregard substantive differences in an effort to reveal*

*formal equivalences.* Thus, for example, in *The Fine Line*, I note the striking parallels between the supposedly discrete chunks of space (neighborhoods), time (weeks), and identity (ethnic groups) into which we sociomentally transform otherwise continuous stretches of reality.[33] By the same token, in *Hidden in Plain Sight*, effectively disregarding the conventional distinction between what we inattend to perceptually (as being "in the background") and conceptually (as being "irrelevant"), I likewise note surgeons' and mathematicians' parallel tendency to decontextualize as well as landscape designers' and social workers' contrasting, parallel heightened attention to context.[34]

In a similar fashion, in *Taken for Granted*, I note parallels between formally analogous contrasting pairs of culturally marked and unmarked acts:

> As so aptly captured by the colloquial notion of "losing" one's virginity, one's very first sexual intercourse [is] conventionally regarded as actually affecting one's very essence far more than one's seven-hundred-and-fifty-eighth one. And whereas a single marked act such as murdering someone is considered highly salient for identity attribution, even four thousand instances of unmarked ones such as raising one's eyebrows or wiping one's nose are not. In sharp contrast to being identified as a murderer, after all, no one is ever identified as an "eyebrow-raiser" or a "nose-wiper."[35]

I also note there the parallels between "retronymic" terms like *acoustic guitar, desktop computer,* and *live music,* each of which would have been semiotically superfluous (and neither of which had therefore indeed even existed) prior to the introduction of the electric guitar, the laptop, and recorded music.[36]

Needless to say, it is not that generic sociologists are actually unable to notice substantive cross-contextual disparities. Yet they purposely disregard them in an effort to uncover formal *cross-contextual parallels.* When analogizing, one thus consciously *disregards conventionally noted differences in order to be able to notice conventionally ignored equivalences.*

That implies opting for "*lumping*" over "splitting,"[37] which presupposes one's epistemic readiness to "foreground" similarities and "background" differences,[38] as one's preferred mode of processing information. In other words, it implies focusing one's attention on the common formal features of a given social pattern across the multiple contexts in which one examines it while purposely disregarding the substantive differences among its various instantiations,[39] which requires, of course, undergoing special attentional socialization, consciously attending to commonalities and disattending disparities.[40]

Language plays a critical role in all this. It is our epistemic ability to assign things a common label, after all, that helps us lump them together in our mind.[41] It is my use of the term *horizon*, for instance, that has helped me notice the striking parallel between the pronouncedly social limits of our intellectual, moral, as well as erotic attention,[42] and it is my use of the term *attentional norms* that has likewise helped me realize that the weeds and bacteria we conventionally deem morally irrelevant are indeed analogous to the events we conventionally consider historically insignificant and thereby collectively forget.[43]

In their social pattern analyses generic sociologists draw on at least one of four major cross-contextual (cross-cultural, cross-historical, cross-domain, and cross-level) types of analogies. Together, those four fundamental forms of analogizing constitute a significant part of their basic epistemic toolkit.

## Cross-Cultural Analogizing

Consider, for starters, the pronouncedly generic-sociological practice of *cross-cultural analogizing*, where one purposely disregards any form of cross-cultural variability in an effort to reveal trans-cultural social patterns. By downplaying the singularity of each of the multiple examples one uses, focusing instead on their commonality, one thus mentally detaches such patterns from the specific cultural contexts in which one actually identifies them, as when Herbert Spencer notes the parallel manner in which Maori, Mexican, Hawaiian, and Fijian priests are functionally differentiated from sorcerers, medical practitioners, diviners, and seers,[44] or when Durkheim notes striking parallels between the French, German, Greek, Roman, Jewish, Chinese, and Egyptian legal systems.[45] Similar *cross-cultural analogies* also play a major role in Mircea Eliade's, Arnold van Gennep's, and Marcel Mauss's respective multi-cultural studies of commemorative festivals, rites of passage, and exchange.[46]

Such analogies likewise help Arie Dubnov note the parallel politics of ethnic partition in Palestine and the Indian Subcontinent in the 1940s,[47] and Iddo Tavory and Daniel Winchester reveal the effectively analogous "experiential careers" of newly religious Jews and new converts to Islam.[48] They also help John Levi Martin uncover the critical role of armed support in Norman, Peruvian, Indian, Polish, East African, and Japanese patronage systems, as well as the strikingly parallel ways of communicating during battle in the Aztec, Chinese, and Carthaginian armies.[49]

My own use of cross-cultural analogies dates back to *The Seven-Day Circle*, where I analyze the strikingly parallel French and Soviet attempts to abolish the seven-day week,[50] and *The Fine Line*, where I uncover the astoundingly similar rigid manner in which Romanies and Orthodox Jews classify reality,[51] yet only in *Time Maps* did I consciously commit myself to cross-cultural analogizing as a special, distinctive theoretico-methodological practice.[52] In an effort to mentally detach the generic and thus transcultural features of collective remembrance from the specific cultural contexts in which I happened to identify them, I therefore purposely downplayed the cultural distinctness (and thus singularity) of each of the examples I used there, focusing instead on their underlying commonality. While Israel/Palestine and Kosovo, for example, constitute two very different contexts for studying collective memory, they nevertheless both exemplify the formal politico-mnemonic discursive strategy of "out-pasting," where two rivaling groups (Arabs and Jews, Albanians and Serbs) both claim exclusive rights to a contested territory by using "our roots here are historically 'deeper' than yours" narratives, thereby disputing the validity of the beginning of each other's narrative as a legitimate point of historical "departure."[53]

While writing that book I read in the newspaper a story about a group of Native American militants who "[w]ith an electric saw . . . severed [the] right foot—boot, stirrup, star-shaped spur and all" of a bronze statue of Juan de Oñate, the Spanish conquistador who in the late 1590s had in fact ordered the right feet of captive Acoma Pueblo Indians who tried to resist his conquest of New Mexico to be chopped off.[54] According to the story, the director of the Oñate Monument and Visitors Center, Estevan Arrellano, was in complete shock: "Give me a break—it was 400 years ago. It's OK to hold a grudge, but for 400 years?"[55] Then, three months later, I happened to read an op-ed piece written by columnist Maureen Dowd, who, having once been chastised by her Irish-American mother for planning to stay in a hotel named after Oliver Cromwell, wryly observed that "in Irish time, 1651 and 1981 were only moments apart."[56] Putting two and two analogically together, I immediately noted the strikingly parallel manner in which even widely disparate cultures may nevertheless hold centuries-old grudges.[57]

In that book I also feature *cross-culturally parallel examples* of politico-discursive manipulation of collective remembering. A classic case in point is the practice of "resetting historical chronometers at zero" in an effort to discursively establish "new beginnings," as coexemplified by France's and Italy's attempts to replace the essentially Christocentric "common" era with pronouncedly politico-centric chronological dating frameworks ("the Republican Era," "the Fascist Era") by effectively substituting the foundation of the French Republic in 1792 and Benito Mussolini's 1922 March on Rome for the birth of Jesus as points of historical "departure," Pol Pot's official designation of 1975, the year he became Cambodia's ruler, as "Year Zero," and the use of the notion of "Zero Hour" in 1945 in an attempt to project Germany's "clean" break with its Nazi past.[58] So, indeed, is the practice of using consecutive ordinal numbers to "bridge over" actual historical gaps, as cross-culturally exemplified by the use of the name "Menelik II" to discursively "link" Ethiopians' late-nineteenth-century emperor to the legendary founder of their kingdom, Menelik I, despite the 2,800-year gap historically separating them from each other, and the effectively parallel manner in which Germany discursively presented its "Third" Reich as the implicitly direct successor of its "Second" empire despite the fifteen-year period (1918–1933) actually separating them from each other.[59]

Elsewhere in the book I also feature cross-culturally parallel efforts to effectively synchronize calendrical and historical time by essentially observing major national holidays on the same date that the historical events they are designed to commemorate actually occurred—Malta's Victory Day on the date of the lifting of the four-month Ottoman siege of the island on September 8, 1565; New Zealand's Waitangi Day on the date of the signing of the historic British–Maori treaty on February 6, 1840; and Colombia's Battle of Boyacá Day on the date of Simón Bolívar's decisive military victory over Spain on August 7, 1819.[60] Furthermore, I also note there the spectacular transcultural socio-mnemonic pattern where many of those events actually form two chronologically distinct clusters respectively representing those nations' ancient spiritual and modern political origins, effectively separated from each other by centuries-long stretches of commemoratively "uneventful," socio-mnemonically "empty" time.[61]

Note, in this regard, that not all the events commemorated now as historically "pivotal" in fact attracted much public attention when they actually occurred. The way Namibians now retrospectively remember the August 26, 1966 shoot-out between South African troops and South West African rebels at Omugulugwombashe as the "watershed"[62] event commemorated annually on Heroes' Day, for example, is a perfect case in point. So, for that matter, is the cross-culturally parallel manner in which the February 21, 1952 student demonstration against the imposition of Urdu as the official language of the predominantly Bengali-speaking province of East Pakistan is collectively remembered now by Bangladeshis as the historically pivotal event commemorated annually on International Mother Language Day. And so, indeed, is also the way Cubans collectively remember now Fidel Castro's July 26, 1953 failed guerrilla attack on the Moncada barracks in Santiago de Cuba, commemorated annually on National Revolution Day, as the actual beginning of what only five and a half years later in fact came to be known as "the Cuban Revolution."[63]

## Cross-Historical Analogizing

As exemplified by the parallels between the Aztec and Carthaginian systems of communicating during battle (which were developed, after all, more than a millennium and a half apart from each other) or the respective introductions of France's "Republican" and Italy's "Fascist" chronological dating frameworks in the 1790s and 1920s, however, some cross-cultural analogies also double as cross-historical ones, as generic sociologists try to uncover not only transcultural social patterns but also transhistorical ones. That implies noting "*historical parallels*" thereby resisting both historians' and sociologists' conventional tendency to valorize historical specificity (that is, to indeed "historicize") and shun such effectively "anachronistic" comparisons.

As an actual theoretico-methodological practice,[64] *cross-historical analogizing* epitomizes such effort to essentially *dehistoricize*. It was their epistemic readiness to analogize, for example, that helped Oswald Spengler note parallel manifestations of "cultural decay" in the third-century Roman, eleventh-century Arab, and early twentieth-century Western worlds,[65] and Theda Skocpol uncover the parallels between the French, Russian, and Chinese revolutions.[66] Their readiness to compare cross-historically analogous "combination[s] of high speed and meager success"[67] likewise helped Eric Hobsbawm, Robert Springborg, and Kurt Weyland note the glaring parallels between the 1848 European "Spring of Nations"[68] and the 2011 "Arab Spring." And it was his readiness to acknowledge the strikingly similar structure of medieval eunuchs' and modern domestic servants' webs of group affiliation that actually allowed Coser to discover the formal social-relational pattern of "undivided commitment."[69]

By the same token, it was my epistemic readiness to resist the conventional tendency to historicize that helped me notice the striking parallel between conservative America's nostalgia toward the 1950s following the social and cultural upheavals of the 1960s and 1970s and the yearning of nineteenth-century Arab historians witnessing the decline of the Ottoman Empire for the past glory of medieval Muslim Spain.[70] It was my readiness to analogize that likewise helped me become aware of the parallel use of the politico-mnemonic tactic of "cutting and pasting" genealogical narratives to help discursively "link" Charlemagne to the Roman Empire in 800 and Iran's Mohammad Reza Shah Pahlavi to the ancient Persian king Cyrus in 1971.[71] And it was my readiness to disregard the obvious historical distinctiveness of the Peloponnesian War, seventeenth-century Puritanism, and the aftermath of World War I that helped me note the strikingly parallel rise of cognitive rigidity during historically separate yet similarly "unsettled"[72] periods of cultural instability.[73]

## Cross-Domain Analogizing

Yet thinking analogically helps the generic sociologist notice parallels across not only space and time but also conventionally distinct, supposedly separate social "domains." Such *cross-domain analogizing*[74] has led Rogers Brubaker, for example, to realize in the summer of 2015 how his "attention was drawn to the pairing of 'transgender' and 'transracial' in debates about whether Caitlyn Jenner could legitimately identify as a woman and Rachel Dolezal as black."[75] While "[g]ender and race are of course 'different differences,'" he agrees, they are nevertheless both "being reimagined, reconstructed, and newly contested in ways that are in some respects strikingly similar."[76]

Although originally dating back to Simmel's assertion in 1908 that one in fact encounters the same fundamental "form[s] of sociation . . . in the state as well as in a religious community, in a band of conspirators as in an economic association, in an art school as in a family,"[77] the most intellectually audacious display of cross-domain analogizing was arguably van Gennep's analysis of the generic, transcontextual properties of the social phenomenon he famously identified as "rites of passage" the very next year. Not only did van Gennep use his classic tripartite schema of separation ("preliminal"), transition ("liminal"), and incorporation ("postliminal") rituals when analyzing actual physical crossings of doorways and national borders,[78] he also applied it to the formally parallel strictly mental "passages" marking the symbolic transitions from pre-birth to infancy, childhood to adulthood, or life to death.[79] A person's life, he noted, is after all sociomentally divided into a supposedly discontinuous series of "stages" effectively separated from one another by putatively "transformative" events such as "birth, social puberty, marriage, fatherhood, advancement to a higher class, occupational specialization, and death," and

> [f]or every one of these events there are ceremonies whose es-
> sential purpose is to enable the individual to pass from one de-
> fined position to another which is equally well defined. Since the
> goal is the same, it follows of necessity that the ways of attaining it
> should be at least *analogous*, if not identical in detail.[80]

Furthermore, he also applied this schema to the formally parallel
envisioned mental "crossings" marking the symbolic acts of "en-
tering" and "exiting" social groups,[81] thereby effectively capturing
humans' social mobility ("passage") in space, time, as well as into
and out of social groups in a single conceptual framework.

As exemplified by Roland Barthes's portrayal of clothes, food,
cars, and furniture as effectively analogous quasi-linguistic systems of signification,[82] such epistemic readiness to disregard substantive differences in an effort to reveal formal parallels across
conventionally separate "domains" is one of the trademarks of the
"structuralist" style of social theorizing. It is thus evident, for example, in Roman Jakobson and Linda Waugh's analogical extension
of Nikolai Trubetzkoy's strictly phonological notion of markedness
into a broader semiotic one,[83] in Ray Birdwhistell's analysis of the
fundamental parallels between speech and nonverbal communication,[84] as well as in Claude Lévi-Strauss's observation that, when
studying kinship systems,

> the anthropologist finds himself in a situation which *formally*
> *resembles* that of the structural linguist. . . . Although they belong
> to another order of reality, kinship phenomena are *of the same*
> *type* as linguistic phenomena. Can the anthropologist, using a
> method *analogous in form* . . . to the method used in structural
> linguistics, achieve the same kind of progress in his own science
> as that which has taken place in linguistics?[85]

It is likewise evident in Kenneth Pike's use of the same conceptual
framework to analyze the phenomenological structure of a church

service and a football game[86] as well as in Edmund Leach's discussion of the strikingly similar taboos surrounding both food and sex objects culturally deemed too "close" to or too "distant" from us.[87] *Noticing formal parallels presupposes an epistemic readiness to disregard substantive differences.* It was their readiness to disregard any differences between substantively disparate "domain"-specific instances of nonetheless analogous patterns, for example, that helped Peter Blau note the parallel social insulation of senators from their constituents and Nobel laureates from ordinary scientists,[88] James Moody and Douglas White reveal formal parallels between high-school friendship networks and interlocking directorates of large firms,[89] and Coser realize that leader–follower relations in youth gangs and scout troops are in fact structurally identical.[90] Such readiness has likewise helped Ivan Chase note the parallel manner in which Methodist ministers and state police officers gain new positions,[91] Vaughan uncover the parallel failure of air-traffic controllers and pre-breakup couples to notice warning signs,[92] and Chancer reveal strikingly similar "sadomasochistic" power dynamics at home and at work.[93]

Cross-domain analogizing has also helped Helen Ebaugh uncover parallel patterns of "role exit" among widows, ex-cons, recovered alcoholics, and retirees,[94] and Barbara Katz Rothman compare the birth and food movements' effectively parallel campaigns against industrialization.[95] It has likewise helped Stephen Reysen and Nyla Branscombe note fundamental parallels between jazz, sport, and science-fiction fans,[96] and Christy Ponticelli reveal glaringly similar patterns of identity construction among religious converts and former lesbians.[97]

My own use of *cross-domain analogies* dates back to *The Fine Line* (which I fittingly subtitled *Making Distinctions in Everyday Life*), where, inspired by van Gennep, I note the striking parallels between the mental fences ("boundaries") we envision separating (and thereby helping distinguish), for example, Kansas from Nebraska, "the sixties" from "the seventies," "sociologists" from "anthropologists," and appropriate from inappropriate behavior. I thus discuss there, for instance, the effectively analogous "liminal" and thereby also ambiguous status of fiancés, presidents-elect, and prisoners on parole,[98] the parallel name-change rituals designed to dramatize the considerable discontinuities we are socially expected to envision between brides' and converts' old and new selves,[99] as well as the substantively disparate yet glaringly analogous manifestations of elites' efforts to substantiate the mental separation of "high" from "popular" culture in order to help differentiate themselves from "the masses":

> It is the essentially purist wish to establish such a mental chasm that leads them to cultivate and passionately defend aesthetic distinctions between "refined" and "vulgar" books (*Madame Bovary* versus *Valley of the Dolls*), films (a Bergman movie versus *Rambo III*), stores (Saks Fifth Avenue versus Kmart), vacation sites (Martha's Vineyard versus Atlantic City), topics of conversation (postmodernism versus garage sales), food (sushi versus hot dogs), drinks (cognac versus beer), cars (Saab versus Ford), newspapers (*Wall Street Journal* versus *National Enquirer*), music (Debussy versus Ray Coniff), television personalities (Bill Moyers versus Johnny Carson), and sports (squash versus bowling).[100]

By the same token, I note the strikingly parallel manner in which we use space to help substantiate the essentially abstract and therefore somewhat vague distinctions we make between the formal and the informal (such as by having separate "living" and "family" rooms), the masculine and the feminine (such as by placing men's and women's clothing on separate floors of department stores), supposedly different "kinds" of information (such as by placing dance- and gymnastics-related news in separate "Arts" and "Sports" newspaper sections), as well as between supposedly different "kinds" of food (such as by placing them in separate aisles of supermarkets, chapters of cookbooks, and sections of the refrigerator).[101] And when discussing the fundamental contrast between cognitive rigidity and flexibility,[102] I likewise stress the latter's use of a "both/ and" (in sharp contrast to the former's "either/or") logic regardless of whether I might choose at some later point to feature the Swiss Army knife, the progressive lens, the Transformer toy, or the retractable dog leash, all of which I consider essentially analogous brainchildren of "the flexible mind," as its prime example.

The practice of analogizing across conventionally disparate, supposedly separate social "domains" has since played a major role in the way I theorize. Thus, for example, in *Hidden in Plain Sight*, I note the substantively disparate yet attentionally parallel efforts to conduct a successful air search for shipwreck survivors, detect a lung tumor on an X-ray, and find a paper clip in a cluttered kitchen drawer,[103] while purposely disregarding the differences between equally "canonical" must-read academic texts and must-see tourist destinations.[104] I likewise compare essentially parallel cosmetic (scar-concealing), hunting ("invisible," odorless), and social (blending-in) "background-matching" techniques,[105] as well as stage magicians', politicians', and pickpockets' strikingly similar diversionary tactics.[106] By the same token, I also note psychotherapists', soccer forwards', and aerial stereoscopic photograph interpreters' effectively analogous "attentional habits,"[107] as well as the parallel "attentional taboos" compelling jurors to disregard legally inadmissible evidence and employers to exclude applicants' age, gender, race, and marital status from their formal hiring considerations.[108]

I also use cross-domain analogies in *Time Maps*, comparing, for example, Muslims' "religious" pilgrimages to Mecca, Americans' "patriotic" visits to Philadelphia's Independence Hall, and couples' "romantic" revisits to the site of their first date as strikingly parallel ritualized efforts to invoke "origin" narratives.[109] And in *The Elephant in the Room* I likewise compare interactions between terminal patients and their doctors and those between military officials who "don't ask" and gay soldiers who "don't tell" in an effort to uncover the generic, transdomain features of conspiracies of silence.[110]

By the same token, in *Ancestors and Relatives*, I consciously disregard the differences between the various "domain"-specific examples of genealogical patterns I use in my analysis. I thus note, for example, the way we analogically extend our imagery of "bloodlines"[111] to further envision dynastic "lines" of academic, artistic, and spiritual mentors and students as well as of successive musical directors, presidents, and popes.[112] I likewise note that the way Roman Catholics view their Church as the actual "trunk" of Christianity's symbolic family tree, thereby essentially "marginalizing"[113] all the other Christian denominations as mere "side branches," actually resembles the way the Soviet Communist Party used to portray Trotskyites, or the way strictly Freudian psychoanalysts often portray Jungian analysts, as having betrayed the true spirit, and thereby effectively disqualified themselves from being considered the true successors, of their common symbolic ancestor (Lenin, Freud).[114]

Similarly, in *Taken for Granted*, their distinctive "domain"-specific features notwithstanding, I purposely disregard the differences between maleness, whiteness, straightness, and able-bodiedness, focusing instead on their all being culturally un-marked, supposedly "normal" social identities conventionally taken for granted and thereby assumed by default. To complement that, I likewise highlight the striking parallels between femaleness, non-whiteness, homosexuality, and disability in an effort to reveal the generic, transcontextual features of markedness. Together, both strategies help reveal the asymmetrical manner in which we tend to envision the pronouncedly contrasting social definitions of identity respectively involved in being male and female, white and non-white, straight and gay, and able-bodied and disabled.[115]

Furthermore, using such cross-domain analogies also helps me reveal striking parallels between supposedly disparate "domain"-specific efforts to epistemically subvert (whether politically, academically, artistically, or comically)[116] the conventional semiotic asymmetry between the culturally marked and unmarked by unmarking the former or marking the latter. I thus compare, for example, the parallel efforts to unmark such terms as "*gay* marriage" and "best *female* tennis player,"[117] as well as the effectively analogous use of the terms *white pride* and *straight pride* by white nationalists and anti-gay activists[118] and the parallel attempts to place the conventionally "normal," culturally unmarked referents of the terms *neurotypical, cisgender,* and *vanilla sex* on an equal semiotic footing with their marked, abnormalized counterparts, which are conventionally labeled *autistic, transgender,* and *kinky.*[119]

One of the pillars of generic theorizing, cross-domain analogizing involves reversing sociologists' (and, for that matter, anthropologists')[120] common tendency to highlight variability. In other words, it implies an effort to *uncover formal parallels across situations conventionally considered fundamentally "different" from one another.*

As a teacher, I thereby try to sensitize my students to cross-contextual parallels, and their epistemic readiness to analogize across conventionally "different" social "domains" is indeed a trademark of their work.[121] Consciously disregarding the differences between hacktivists and hooded Klansmen in an effort to uncover the generic, transcontextual properties of anonymity,[122] DeGloma, for example, thus notes,

> I explore a variety of cases to demonstrate how anonymity is used to protect individuals from various discreditable acts. . . . Such a function of anonymity is evident in the ethic of the screened confessional. It is also . . . an important rationale for allowing anonymous media sources, and a core justification for providing anonymous tip lines for solving crimes or conveying information to authorities. Further, the protective character of anonymity is evident in nameless exam grading and teacher evaluation practices, the use of tinted windows on automobiles and two-way

mirrors during police lineups, and with the blurring of bystander faces in film and video.[123]

Cross-domain analogizing also helps Wayne Brekhus view military bases, ethnic enclaves, monasteries, and student dorms as but effectively parallel "identity-specific spaces,"[124] Samantha Spitzer note the strikingly similar phenomenological properties of cancer remissions, post-earthquakes, and terrorist sleeper cells as dormant yet ever-lurking threats,[125] and Johanna Foster uncover the parallel politics of intersexual and biracial in-betweenness.[126] It likewise helps Christena Nippert-Eng note the glaringly parallel interruptibility of women at home and in the workplace,[127] Rachelle Germana compare the double (both connecting and separating) semiotic function of hyphenation in the contexts of familial ("Day-Lewis") and ethnic ("Italian-American") identity,[128] and Jenna Howard uncover the effectively parallel manner in which recovering "alcoholics," "anorexics," and "agoraphobics," for example, "disidentify" with their formerly embraced clinical labels.[129]

Needless to say, it is not that Howard is actually unable to notice differences between alcoholics and anorexics, just as Mullaney is fully aware of the differences between abstaining from dairy products, illegal drugs, and sex. Nevertheless, she consciously lumps them together as but various examples of "recovery identities."[130] As she describes the theoretico-methodological logic of cross-domain analogizing,

> I analytically lump together labels as diverse as "codependent," "bulimic," "bipolar," and "schizophrenic," and I intentionally disattend the often significant symptomatic differences between these different labels. *Looking at these disparate identities with a focus on their analytic similarities* is helpful in my effort to formally highlight *generic* temporal patterns in the narratives. Certainly, the emotional disorder experience is influenced by the

type and severity of symptoms, but I *intentionally overlook this diversity.*[131]

## Cross-Level Analogizing

To allow for generic theorizing, not only does social pattern analysis involve cross-cultural, cross-historical, and/or cross-domain analogizing, it may also require one's epistemic readiness to disregard the differences between the micro-, meso-, and macrosocial instantiations of a given social pattern in an effort to uncover formal "regularities that do not respect . . . levels of [social] aggregation."[132] Maintaining such conscious *indifference to scale* implies noting, for instance, that our homophilic tendency to associate with those who are "like" us manifests itself quite similarly at both the individual and group levels,[133] that "impression-management" tactics work somewhat similarly at both the interpersonal and international levels,[134] that the experience of living as if on a besieged island is strikingly similar whether the envisioned "island" happens to be a small settlement, a large city, or an entire country,[135] and that the very same dynamics of inclusion and exclusion evidently operate at the levels of the body, the home, and the state.[136]

*Cross-level analogizing* has thus helped me notice the remarkably similar manner in which families may collude to ignore (thereby effectively "co-denying") members' addiction and entire nations may refuse to acknowledge the glaring incompetence of their leader,[137] as well as the strikingly parallel, fundamentally genealogical foundations of families, ethnic groups, ethno-nations, and species:[138]

> Although conventionally considered distinct from one another, families, ethno-nations, and species are actually all based on the genealogical principle of co-descent. The ties we envision connecting cousins, fellow Norwegians, and penguins, for example,

are thus strikingly similar, and the very same logic underlies both family and evolutionary trees. We are essentially dealing here with one and the same principle of genealogical connectivity evidently manifesting itself at many different levels of social aggregation.[139]

Drawing *cross-level analogies* has likewise helped me become aware of the unmistakably similar role of weddings and naturalization ceremonies in institutionally substantiating ultimately imaginary "crossings" of familial and national boundaries[140] as well as realize that setting statutes of limitations at a state level bears a striking resemblance to the way friends choose to "let bygones be bygones."[141] Only "the analogical imagination,"[142] indeed, allows one to actually disregard the differences, and thereby become aware of the remarkable parallels, between familial and national "co-denial," ethnic groups and species, getting married and becoming a naturalized citizen, and setting statutes of limitations and letting bygones be bygones.

# 5

# Eureka!

[C]omputers can only dream with impatience of that far-off day when they, too, will at last be able to perceive that two situations so different on their surface level are nonetheless "exactly the same thing."

—Douglas Hofstadter and Emmanuel Sander,
*Surfaces and Essences*, 115

While making the case for generic theorizing, it has definitely not been my intent here to disparage other (ethnographic, historical) forms of social inquiry that are specifically designed to highlight the singularity of culturally or historically specific situations or events. Having actually even used them in my own work,[1] I am well aware of the considerable methodological benefits they offer sociologists.

Indeed, it is important to examine *both* the way in which two situations are similar to *and* the way in which they are different from each other. Theorizing the generic, in other words, need not really replace the study of the specific.

## From "No-Nos" to Methodological Virtues

Theorizing generically (and, as such, also transcontextually), of course, inevitably raises the epistemic danger of developing "tunnel vision"[2] thereby figuratively taking things "out of context." Being

*Generally Speaking*. Eviatar Zerubavel, Oxford University Press (2021). © Oxford University Press.
DOI: 10.1093/oso/9780197519271.001.0001.

"focused," in other words, thus involves the use of a metaphorical scalpel[3] that necessarily violates the integrity of our phenomenal experience. "When analytic thought, the knife, is applied to experience," as Robert Pirsig so evocatively put it, "something is always killed in the process."[4]

Furthermore, it is also quite clear what we lose by opting for a "thick analysis and thin but widely spread description of social settings that reveal the analytic principles being studied" over a "thick description and thin but widely spread analysis of a specific social setting so that it is understood in all its contours and details,"[5] to use Brekhus's colorful imagery. After all, the further we move toward studying the general and therefore also less concrete, the less we are able to capture the rich "texture" (that is, "all [the] contours and details") of groups, situations, and events we can do so effectively when using ethnographic or historical forms of inquiry, which are specifically designed, of course, to highlight singularity. By choosing to analytically "zoom out" on the general, in other words, we thus inevitably deprive ourselves of the opportunity to capture the descriptively "thick," richly textured singularity and thereby distinctness of the particular.

When thinking in generalities, there is always also the danger of "overgeneralizing." By the same token, when drawing analogies, we are likewise confronted with the perennial epistemic challenge of avoiding making the "false equivalences" alluded to by the often-heard complaint "How can you even compare them?"[6]

Yet while being fully aware of the epistemic cost of figuratively blinding ourselves to context[7] and thereby also to singularity, I am equally cognizant of what we actually gain by choosing to do so. After all, just as epistemically dangerous as the problem of overgeneralizing is the diametrically opposite problem of *undergeneralizing*,[8] so aptly captured in the metaphorical image of being "unable to see the forest for the trees." Without a "theory of trans-situational, trans-cultural, and trans-historical relevance," indeed, we thus "unduly limit the explanatory potential of socio-logical inquiry."[9]

Thus, for example, when we narrowly regard studies we conduct *in* particular settings as studies *of* those settings,[10] we may not realize that we are actually dealing with but specific instantiations of generic, transcontextual social patterns.[11] It was anthropologists' traditional tendency to undergeneralize, for instance, that kept Edward Evans-Pritchard from realizing that his analysis of the Nuer kinship system[12] actually demonstrates the centrality of the principle of "co-descent" to *any* genealogical system.[13]

By contrast, it was his unmistakable epistemic readiness to transcend singularity, indeed, that enabled Pasteur to extend Edward Jenner's ideas about vaccination beyond the particular context of smallpox and thereby envision its potential use in preventing other infectious diseases as well.[14] And it was that very readiness to transcend singularity, after all, that likewise enabled Goffman to extend his analysis of the social interaction patterns he observed in the Shetland Islands beyond that specific setting and famously produce *The Presentation of Self in Everyday Life* rather than *The Presentation of Self in the Shetlands*.

Effectively enhanced by modern academic *overspecialization*, as evidenced by the relentless proliferation of increasingly parochial subspecialties, our tendency to undergeneralize is in fact professionally induced. Yet as I try to demonstrate by deliberately disregarding the conventional academic separation of the specific research areas respectively explored by students of kinship, ethnicity, nationhood, and race from one another when writing in *Ancestors and Relatives* about genealogical communities and identities, only by thinking transcontextually can scholars in any subspecialty benefit from essentially "parallel" research done in others.[15]

Such epistemic challenge is even more daunting, of course, when one considers institutionally distinct, conventionally "different" disciplines, as so strikingly exemplified by the total unawareness that the schematic diagrams traditionally used by social anthropologists to depict lineage segmentation are almost identical to the ones traditionally used by historical linguists as well as molecular biologists to respectively portray the genealogical divergence of English from Dutch as well as humans from apes.[16] The increasing *compartmentalization* of modern academic knowledge has thus effectively kept members of those three institutionally separate and therefore supposedly "different" disciplines from realizing that they have in fact all been dealing with but various specific manifestations of one and the same transcontextual genealogical principle, namely co-descent. Only by deliberately disregarding the conventional, utterly artificial boundaries separating different disciplinary "fields" (and thus also supposedly different and thereby separate "literatures") from one another and therefore impeding *intellectual cross-fertilization*, indeed, can we actually become aware of the strikingly parallel genealogical ties "connecting" us to our siblings, fellow co-ethnics, and baboons.[17]

Only by being willing to lose specificity, in other words, can we gain epistemic access to genericity. And only by deliberately *decontextualizing* our findings, indeed, can we figuratively "distill" generic, transcontextual social patterns from the specific contexts in which we actually identify them, and which we would have most likely missed altogether had we focused instead on the singularity of those contexts.

It was thinking transcontextually, after all, that in fact enabled me to develop in *Time Maps* a pronouncedly generic-sociological perspective on the way we narrate the past. Only by using the very same conceptual framework to capture the way we try to legitimize our claims to library carrels, parking spots, as well as homelands by insisting that we were there "first," for instance, could I generically theorize the phenomenon of "out-pasting."[18] And only by examining the politics of remembrance at both the micro- and macrosocial levels could I note the glaringly parallel manner in which couples as well as entire nations construct their collective "origins."[19]

By the same token, only by actually focusing on the generic, transcontextual properties of conspiracies of silence and consciously disregarding scale, as I in fact did when writing *The Elephant in the Room*, can one note the strikingly similar manner in which families, organizations, as well as entire societies "co-deny" the presence of "elephants" in their midsts. Yet when no attempt is made to transcend the singularity of such situations and view them as but various instantiations of one and the same formal, transcontextual social pattern, the spectacular lack of dialogue between those who study familial "open secrets" and those who study corporate or national ones is indeed hardly surprising.[20]

In using focusing, generalizing, and analogical exampling as my main theoretico-methodological tactics, however, I am essentially ignoring, of course, some major conventional epistemic "no-nos" given which I may very well be accused of taking things "out of context," "overgeneralizing," and making "false equivalences." Yet I actually do so quite deliberately, regarding such "sins," indeed, as methodological virtues.

Thus, for example, I purposely *dis*attend (rather than inadvertently *in*attend to)[21] the distinctive features of any specific community, situation, or event I examine[22] in an effort to "distill" from it certain generic, transcontextual social patterns, just as I disregard the difference between acute and obtuse triangles in order to lay bare their common triangularity. I likewise purposely confine my attention to only certain aspects of that community, situation, or event,[23] attributing my decision to ignore all its other aspects to my conscious effort to stay "focused" rather than to the practical impossibility of studying "everything." Confining my scholarly concern to only those thematically preselected aspects thereby deliberately disregarding others thus exemplifies how, far from being the result of some epistemic oversight, the concept-driven-sociological practice of approaching social communities, situations, or events selectively is indeed part of a full-fledged, deliberate theoretico-methodological agenda.

## Analogical Transfers

Given sociologists' general tendency to epistemically privilege differences over similarities, efforts to encourage young practitioners to analogize, as exemplified by the following attempt to make one's students aware of the strikingly parallel politico-semiotic properties of maleness, whiteness, and straightness,[24] are particularly laudable:

> I want my students to understand that men are gendered too. . . . To let the study of gender be equivalent to the study of women is to leave men as unmarked by gender and hence normatively human. . . . Once they have internalized this model, a study of race . . . can no longer be mistaken solely for a study of people of color. Students will now come to see whites as being raced as well. Further . . . they come to see that the commonly posed question "What causes homosexuality?" . . . takes as norm and leaves uninterrogated the dominant category of heterosexuality.[25]

Yet analogizing also takes the form of extracting concepts from the specific contexts in which they are conventionally used and *extrapolating* their connotational potential to others,[26] as exemplified by extending the semantic scope of the term *trauma* from physical to psychological injury and of the term *racism* to its phonetic cousins *sexism, ageism, classism,* and *ableism,* or by the ludic use of the labels *Travelgate, Zippergate,* and *Bridgegate* in reference to post-Watergate political scandals. Thinking analogically thus involves "transferring" the connotation of a given concept to a conventionally separate domain, such as from drinking (*alcoholic*) to work (*workaholic*), from medicine (*recovering patient*) to religion (*recovering Catholic*), or from work (*non-practicing lawyer*) to both politics (*non-practicing Republican*) and sex (*non-practicing virgin*).

To appreciate the potential intellectual benefits of such *analogical transfers*,[27] consider, for example, Weber's and Berger's respective efforts to extrapolate the ultimately religious concepts of charisma and conversion to politics,[28] or Pierre Bourdieu's effort to extrapolate the term *capital* from the strictly economic to the cultural (and particularly symbolic) domain.[29] By the same token, consider also Garfinkel's, Abigail Saguy's, and Laura Enriquez's efforts to respectively extend the transgressive connotation of the term *passing* beyond the context of race to gender, sexual orientation, and undocumented immigration,[30] as well as Susan Stryker's attempt to extrapolate the prefix *trans-* beyond the domain of gender to the conventionally separate yet nonetheless sociopolitically parallel domain of race:

> To say that *transracial* is not "like" *transgender* merely highlights how impoverished our conceptual vocabulary truly is, for specifying modes of resemblance . . . for clearly there are underlying similarities . . . which we have yet to adequately map. An actual point of connection between race and sex is that both name cultural processes that transform physical attributes of bodily being—phenotypes, on the one hand, and morphology and reproductive potential, on the other—into guarantors of social positionality: they are mechanisms for hierarchizing differences . . . through a set of beliefs and practices about the meaning of the material body. . . . It is this shared grounding in a particular biopolitical strategy for managing bodies politic through the inculcation of individual biologized identities that provides a real basis for comparing sex and race, as well as for comparing the stories we might tell about the potential for . . . transfers and transformations of kinds and types of personhood within these categories.[31]

Yet our ability to extend the pronouncedly personalistic connotation of the term *charisma* beyond the domain of religion is by no
means confined to Weber's effort to extrapolate it only to the domain of politics. After all, it has certainly proved to be at least as
equally extrapolatable to the domains of both music (Elvis Presley)
and sport (Muhammad Ali), just as the essentially statistical term
*minority* is often extrapolated to also include women, who are certainly not a statistical minority in the general population. Nor, for
that matter, has the use of the term *intersectionality* been confined,
as it was initially, to the relations between race and gender,[32] as
evidenced by various attempts to extend it to the relations between
each of them and both class and sexuality.

Consider also, in this regard, the tremendous potential advantage of extrapolating the term *one-drop rule* beyond the specific
context of race, where one figurative "drop" of marked blackness
genealogically outweighs an entire "ocean"[33] of unmarked whiteness,[34] to connote a general, transcontextual "one-drop mindset"
characterized by a purist aversion to any "drop" of impurity. Such a
mindset, notes Brekhus, "assumes deviance with the slightest hint
of evidence"[35] thereby

> avoid[ing] ambiguities or in-between identities because it pushes
> those who have even a "traceable amount" of perversion into the
> category of "full-fledged perverts." Following this rule, there is no
> such thing as a "partial pervert." A woman seen turning tricks at
> a busy intersection is defined not as 1/20th of a prostitute . . . but
> simply as a "prostitute" . . . even if only 1 in 20 of her sexual
> interactions . . . involve[s] the exchange of money.[36]

In a similar vein, even a single same-sex encounter may be enough
to taint one's identity as straight. Indeed, as tacitly implied by the
inclusion of the letter "B" in the initialisms *LGBT* and *LGBTQ*, despite the fact that bisexuality is actually a blend of *both* homo- and
heterosexual tendencies, bisexual individuals tend to be lumped

with homosexual rather than heterosexual ones.[37] By the same logic, within such "one-drop mindset," even a tiny speck of meat may ruin an otherwise vegetarian dish, while someone caught lying even once may very well be considered "a liar."

Consider also, along similar lines, the extension of the use of the image of the figurative closet and the acts of both "coming out" of it and "outing" those hiding within it beyond the context of homosexuality. The tremendous potential advantage of such extension has been quite evident ever since John Kitsuse first used the term *coming out* in reference to both physically disabled persons and rape victims,[38] references later further extended by Saguy (along with Anna Ward and Enriquez) to fat persons,[39] Mormon polygamists,[40] and undocumented immigrants,[41] and

> [a] search for the terms *coming out* and *closet* in the keywords of major papers . . . yields examples of people coming out as asexual, celibates, male heterosexuals, Jews, Republicans, Scots, Kiwi males, witches (coming out of "broom closets"!), shopaholics, minivan aficionados, slackers, knitters, homemakers, Christian musicians, and men with erectile dysfunction.[42]

Similar analogical transfers help us realize that the way gay people disclose their culturally marked identity actually resembles the way vegetarians,[43] for instance, disclose theirs, while the striking parallels between the acts of "outing" gay celebrities, sexual predators,[44] undercover agents, and whistleblowers help reveal the generic, transcontextual properties of forced publicity.

Yet the greatest theoretico-methodological advantage analogizing offers generic sociologists is the ability to extrapolate not only concepts but also actual social patterns from one particular context to others. Freeing the process of sociological theorizing "of the peculiarities of some one time and place" thus allows us to identify "many situations in various parts of the world comparable to those that originally aroused [our] interest."[45] Someone interested in bargaining, for example, can thereby gain insights from studying negotiations between landlords and tenants into ones involving parents and children, while someone interested in international conflict resolution may find it useful to also examine marital disputes or barroom scuffles.[46] By the same token, "[i]f we can discern *parallels across contexts* in the way people compete for and respond to assignments of rank, then insights derived from behavior in one context can be applied . . . in others."[47] Thus, for example, points out Coser,

> [a]lthough there is little similarity between the behavior displayed at the court of Louis XIV and that displayed in the main offices of an American corporation, a study of the forms of subordination and superordination in each will reveal *underlying patterns common to both*. On a concrete and descriptive level, there would seem little connection between the early psychoanalytic movement in Vienna and the early Communist movement, but attention to typical forms of interaction among the members of these groups reveals that both are importantly shaped by the fact that they have the structural features of the sect.[48]

Indeed, the very idea of conducting transcontextual research rests on the assumption that we can actually "learn something about any group" or social setting "by *examining similar processes in any other setting*."[49]

Indeed, as I realized while writing *Time Maps*, being cognizant of the manipulative manner in which companies portray their collective past in their publicity brochures also helped me become more aware of the strikingly parallel manipulative aspects of the way nation-states narrate theirs in their national museums and history textbooks.[50] Yet analogical transfers are often bidirectional, thereby actually offering us insight into *both* "source" and "target" analogs[51] rather than only into the latter. Being aware of the distinction between "primary" and "secondary" signifiers of race (such as between skin color and slang), for example, thus also helps us become more aware of the parallel distinction between those of gender (such as between genitals and clothes)[52] *as well as vice versa.* That is also true of similar transfers between the identities "binational" and "biracial" as well as between the essentially parallel acts of traversing national and gender boundaries by immigrants and transgender people, thereby possibly also promoting intellectual cross-fertilization[53] between students of immigration and of gender.

The tremendous theoretico-methodological potential of such *bidirectional analogical transfers*[54] underlies Hughes's very vision of a generic, transcontextual sociology of work:

> [T]he essential problems of men at work are the same whether they do their work in the laboratories of some famous institution or in the messiest vat room of a pickle factory. Until we can find a point of view and concepts which will enable us to make comparisons between the junk peddler and the professor . . . we cannot do our best work in this field.
>
> Perhaps there is as much to be learned about the high-prestige occupations by applying to them the concepts which naturally come to mind for study of people in the most lowly kinds of work as there is to be learned by applying to other occupations the conceptions developed in connection with the highly valued professions.[55]

"The comparative student of . . . work," he therefore notes, "learns about doctors by studying plumbers" (as both exemplify our personal need to trust others to handle our emergencies) as well as "about prostitutes by studying psychiatrists" (as both exemplify the professional need "not to become too personally involved with clients who come to them with rather intimate problems"), thus revealing the generic features of *all* kinds of work "regardless of their places in prestige or ethical ratings."[56]

## Diving Beneath the Social Surface

It was thinking analogically, indeed, that helped me notice the striking parallel between setting statutes of limitations and "letting bygones be bygones." It likewise helped me become aware of the parallel rise in the amounts of academic attention paid to maleness, whiteness, and straightness in the 1980s and 1990s,[57] as well as of the historical coincidence of numerous substantively disparate instantiations of a consciously non-rigid manner of classifying:

> Multinational corporations and global communication networks are distinct[ly] modern phenomena. So are . . . the work[s] of Cage, Magritte, Cummings, and Barth. Nor is it a coincidence that Dada, cubism . . . and the collage are all products of the same generation (the one that also produced . . . Pirandello and Mondrian) or that the "happening" . . . unisex fashion, the "open school" (with its movable walls, flexible schedules, unstructured curriculum, and flexible age-grouping), "open marriage," and Eastern mysticism all flourished in America around the same time. The historical coincidence of such a wide variety of cultural phenomena suggests that they are *more closely interrelated than might appear at first glance.* Indeed, they are all expressions of all-embracing attempts to blur distinctions and obliterate barriers. *The very same attitude* toward boundaries underlies the holistic critique of the medical compartmentalization of our body into supposedly insular systems, the animal-rights movement, community mental health, environmental art, and poststructuralism. They are but different . . . *products of the same basic* modern effort to destroy the ossified order promoted by the rigid mind.[58]

Thinking analogically presupposes *bisociation*, a mental process most elegantly described by Arthur Koestler as "*perceiving a situation or event in . . . habitually incompatible associative contexts*"[59] and thus tacitly reminding us that such "incompatibility" is merely habitual. And since habit is effectively antithetical to creativity, such ability to fuse or combine[60] is essential to being creative. As William James, indeed, characterized the epistemic readiness to note similarities between supposedly "different" entities,

> the crude fact remains, that *some people are far more sensitive to resemblances, and far more ready to point out wherein they consist, than others are.* They are the wits, the poets, the inventors, the scientific men, the practical geniuses. *A native talent for perceiving analogies* is reckoned . . . as *the leading fact in genius of every order.*[61]

The classic example of bisociation on which Koestler's very notion of "the act of creation"[62] is indeed modeled is Archimedes's famous "Eureka moment," which involved mentally fusing the sight of the rise of the water level as he entered the bath with his ongoing effort to calculate the proportion of gold in the royal crown.[63] Just as illustrative in this regard were the role of the increasingly ubiquitous presence of the mechanical pump in William Harvey's discovery of the circulation of blood[64] and the *"Resemblances"* noted by Sigmund Freud *"between the Psychic Lives of Savages and Neurotics."*[65]

The *mental fusion of "different" things* plays a critical role in scientific discovery,[66] where one of the most formidable epistemic challenges one faces, indeed, is realizing "that two things are 'the same thing'" even when "their sameness has not yet been seen."[67] This is certainly true of generic sociologists, who try to mentally connect things that "while found in different parts of the social world and perhaps even known to participants in other terms, nevertheless share identical formal properties,"[68] thereby revealing hidden "commonalities . . . that exist despite the appearance of difference."[69]

"An analogy's power," claim Hofstadter and Sander, "comes from the fact that it *sees beyond the surface differences* of two situations to reveal something *deep and hidden* they have in common."[70] Drawing on the surface and depth metaphors, they thus characterize the act of analogizing as one of mentally connecting situations that "*seem* remote when only their surface is taken into account"[71] yet nevertheless "share a conceptual skeleton at a *deeper level.*"[72]

"Differences," as we are reminded by Ralph Waldo Emerson, are often merely *superficial.*[73] Given the fundamental contrast between "surface" (that is, superficial) appearances[74] and "*underlying*"[75] realities (those figuratively "lying under" the surface), we may therefore need to effectively disregard them. Our ability to in fact do so is made possible, of course, by our minds, those "powerful engines built to seek *hidden, deep commonalities*"[76] by using analogies to figuratively dive beneath the surface in an effort to *uncover* and *reveal* what actually lies there.

Such epistemic "dives" also provide generic theorizers with quasi-aesthetic intellectual pleasure. It is "the pleasure which the mind derives from *the perception of similitude in dissimilitude,*" which, as William Wordsworth so wisely put it, "is the great spring of the activity of our minds, and their chief feeder."[77]

Only by disregarding "surface" differences between *seemingly disparate* instantiations of what is in fact one and the same social pattern can we actually uncover fundamental formal (and thereby transcontextual) commonalities among them.[78] And there, in a nutshell, lies the great promise of concept-driven, generic sociology.

# Notes

## Chapter 1

1. For some earlier, partial attempts to do so, see Zerubavel 1980; Zerubavel 2007.
2. Durkheim 1982 [1895]. See also Max Weber's unmistakably theoretical yet nevertheless aptly titled *The Methodology of the Social Sciences* (1949 [1903–17]).
3. See also Zerubavel 1980, 32.
4. Burawoy 2009, 13. Emphasis added.
5. Blumer 1969, 24–25. Emphasis added.
6. Zerubavel 1979, xv.
7. See, for example, Charmaz 2014, 6.
8. See also Zerubavel 1980, 28–29; Hanemaayer 2009, 158; Nippert-Eng 2015, 36. See also Dyson 1997, 50 on "concept-driven scientific revolutions."
9. Zerubavel 2007. See also Brekhus 2007, 456–59; Friedman 2013, 151–52; DeGloma 2014, 27–28; Mullaney 2019.
10. See also Koningsveld 1973, 5, 12.
11. Zerubavel 1980, 31.
12. Fine 1998, 102. Emphases added.
13. Blumer 1954, 7. See also Blumer 1931, 518, 526–28; Denzin 1970, 14–15; Schwartz and Jacobs 1979, 28; Zerubavel 1980, 26, 31; Van den Hoonaard 1996; Vaughan 2014, 66; Swedberg 2017, 196.
14. See also Glaser 1978, 39; Meyer et al. 2010 on "threshold concepts."
15. On attentional conventions, see Zerubavel 2015, 10, 56, 64.
16. Proust 2006 [1923], 657.
17. Zerubavel 2015, 84.
18. Meyer et al. 2010, ix. Emphasis added.
19. Fleck 1979 [1935], 23–27. See also Elkana 1974, 14, 17.
20. Merton 1984, 267.
21. Fleck 1979 [1935], 23–27.
22. See also Simmel 1950 [1917], 11; Zerubavel 1979, xvi.
23. See also Geertz 1973, 22.

24. Zerubavel 1979, xvii. See also Zerubavel 1985 [1981], x–xi.
25. Zerubavel 1979, xvi–xvii. Emphasis added.
26. Zerubavel 2015, 2.
27. Kuhn 1970 [1962], 126. Emphasis added. See also Fleck 1979 [1935].
28. See also Zerubavel 2015, 24.
29. Davenport and Beck 2001, 60. Emphases added.
30. Neisser 1964, 94.
31. Glaser and Strauss 1971, 183. See also Glaser 1978, 42.
32. See, for example, Glaser and Strauss 1967; Charmaz 2014.
33. Ira Cohen, personal communication.
34. Zerubavel 1979, xvi; Zerubavel 1980, 30–31.
35. Schwartz and Jacobs 1979, 289. Emphases added.
36. Zerubavel 1979, xvi.
37. Zerubavel 1980, 31.
38. Kantorovich 1993, 113. See also Fleck 1979 [1935], 92, 99.
39. Pearce 1912, 941.
40. Ibid., 944.
41. Kuhn 1970 [1962], 116.
42. Zerubavel 1997, 45–46; https://en.wikipedia.org/wiki/List_of_exceptional_asteroids.
43. Zerubavel 1989 [1985], 1.
44. Berger and Luckmann 1967 [1966].
45. Zerubavel 1989 [1985], 138–41; Zerubavel 2016.
46. Zerubavel 2015, ix–x.
47. Garfinkel 1967.
48. See also Zerubavel 1985 [1981], 19–30; Zerubavel 2018.
49. Zerubavel 1979, 27–28, 56, 130.
50. Ibid., 53. See also Zerubavel 1985 [1981], 147–66.
51. Zerubavel 1979, 95–96, 108–09.
52. Zerubavel 1985 [1981], 25.
53. See also ibid., 12–30.
54. Zerubavel 1976.
55. Zerubavel 1979, 60–83.
56. Ibid., 90–91.
57. Ibid., 88–94.
58. Zerubavel 2003, 37–54, 82–100.
59. Zerubavel 2011, 20, 95–97, 120, 126–30.
60. Zerubavel 2018, 1, 4–6, 9, 15, 19.
61. Ibid., 96, 28.

62. Ibid., 59.
63. Zerubavel 1997.
64. Durkheim 1973 [1914].
65. Fleck 1979 [1935], 45, 103.
66. See also Zerubavel 2019.
67. See, for example, Sorokin 1943.
68. See, for example, Zerubavel 1997, 9–10, 54–55, 73–79, 105–08.
69. See, for example, Schutz and Luckmann 1973. See also Berger and Luckmann 1967 [1966].
70. Natalia Ruiz-Junco, personal communication.
71. See, for example, Arendt 1968, 205–06.
72. Zerubavel 2015, 24–27.
73. Ibid., 63–69.
74. Mills 1959.
75. Zerubavel 2015, 64.
76. Collins 1985.
77. Brodsky 1987.
78. Kidahashi 1987.
79. Gricar 1991.
80. Wolfe 1994.
81. Nippert-Eng 1996.
82. Foster 2000.
83. Purcell 2001.
84. Isaacson 2001; Saeki 2017.
85. Chayko 2002.
86. Brekhus 2003.
87. Watson 2005.
88. Simpson 2006.
89. Mullaney 2006.
90. Howard 2008b.
91. Germana 2012.
92. Friedman 2013.
93. DeGloma 2014.
94. Malyk 2014.
95. Yeh 2018.
96. Stein 2019.
97. Battle 2019.
98. Campion 2019.
99. Peña-Alves 2019.

# Chapter 2

1. See also Lofland 1976, 31.
2. See also Tavory and Timmermans 2014, 121.
3. Durkheim 1995 [1912].
4. Weber 2002 [1904].
5. Mead 1934; Parsons 1951; Berger and Luckmann 1967 [1966].
6. Watson 2005, 9.
7. Simmel 1959 [1908], 319.
8. Simmel 1950 [1917], 21–23.
9. See also Simmel 1959 [1908], 320; Simmel 1950 [1917], 21–22; Smith 1989, 31.
10. Glaser and Strauss 1967, 32–35, 79–99; Freese 1980.
11. Blumer 1956, 684–85; McLuhan and Puddephatt 2019. See also Hughes 1971 [1956], 438; Lofland 1976, 31–33, 49–51.
12. Prus 1987, 251; Prus 1996. See also McLuhan and Puddephatt 2019; Puddephatt and McLuhan 2019.
13. Blumer 1956, 685.
14. Schwalbe et al. 2000, 421.
15. See also Snow et al. 2003, 188–89; Rivera et al. 2010, 93.
16. Erikson 2017, 13–15. Emphases added.
17. Zerubavel 1980, 27.
18. Blumer 1931, 520.
19. Hughes 1971 [1956], 438.
20. Simmel 1959 [1908], 316. See also 313.
21. Simmel 1950 [1917], 21.
22. Blumer 1931, 520.
23. Ibid., 515.
24. Ibid., 521. Emphases added.
25. Zerubavel 2007, 132.
26. Levine 1959, 24. Emphasis added.
27. Zerubavel 2016, 73.
28. Zerubavel 2007, 132, 135. See also Davis 1997, 370; Prus 2010, 512, 518, 524; McLuhan and Puddephatt 2019, 84.
29. Lofland 1995, 40; Erikson 2013, 219.
30. Coser 1971, 179.
31. Ibid., 180.
32. Erikson 2005 [1966], xvi. Emphases added.
33. Ibid. Emphasis added. See also Horwitz 1990, 15.

34. See also Prus 1987, 251; Schwalbe et al. 2000, 422; Snow et al. 2003, 188; Prus 2010, 509, 514, 517; McLuhan and Puddephatt 2019, 84.
35. See also Prus 1996, 165.
36. Glaser 1978, 149–50. Emphasis added.
37. Prus 1996, 141–66; Zerubavel 2007, 131, 136; Prus 2010, 507–08, 518, 524. See also Denzin 1970, 15; Brekhus 2007, 456; Rivera et al. 2010, 93; Jutel 2015, 847; McLuhan and Puddephatt 2019, 74; Jutel 2019, 154.
38. Simmel 1959 [1908], 318. See also Coser 1971, 180.
39. Simmel 1959 [1908], 316.
40. Prus 1996, 143. See also Zerubavel 1980; Zerubavel 2007; McLuhan and Puddephatt 2019, 75.
41. Lofland 1976, 39n15; Coser 1994, 1, 4, 11.
42. See also Smith 1989, 22; Coser 1994, 7; Becker 1998, 1.
43. See Zerubavel 2011, 120–21.
44. Zerubavel 1993 [1991].
45. Zerubavel 2003, 30–31.
46. Ibid., 103, 52.
47. Ibid., 9.
48. See, for example, Pollock 2004.
49. See, for example, Jordan 2000.
50. See, for example, Greenwald and Zeitlin 1987.
51. See, for example, Wajnryb 2001.
52. Simmel 1950 [1917], 11.
53. Zerubavel 1993 [1991], 199, 200, 203, 202.
54. Zerubavel 2003, 171, 172, 177, 176.
55. Zerubavel 2006, 160, 157, 158, 162.
56. Zerubavel 2018, 137, 139, 140, 141.
57. See also DeGloma and Papadantonakis 2020.
58. Zerubavel 2003, 37–54, 101–10.
59. Zerubavel 2018, 10–20, 60–91, 32–59.
60. Zerubavel 2006, 47–59, 33–45, 61–72.
61. Zerubavel 2011, 53–75, 77–103, 105–14.
62. See also Zerubavel 2007.

# Chapter 3

1. Margalit 2002, ix.
2. Ibid.

3. See also Lofland 1976, 31; Burawoy 2009, 202.
4. See, for example, Burawoy 2009, 201–02.
5. Wagner-Pacifici 2000.
6. Chancer 2005.
7. Zerubavel 2007, 134–36. See also Jutel 2015, 847; Jutel 2017, 3.
8. Puddephatt and McLuhan 2019, 140. Emphasis added.
9. Kennedy 1979, 665.
10. Ibid. See also Glaser 1978, 145.
11. Zerubavel 1985 [1981], ix–xi.
12. See also Kuran 1995, xi.
13. Brekhus 2007, 457–58. Emphasis added.
14. Zerubavel 2003, 9–10. Emphases added.
15. Zerubavel 2006, 14. Emphases added.
16. Verhoeven 1993, 340. Emphasis added.
17. Prus 1987, 264. Emphasis added. See also Glaser and Strauss 1967, 156.
18. Glaser and Strauss 1971, 186. Emphasis added.
19. Schofield 1990, 212. Emphasis added. See also Burawoy 1998, 25.
20. Hochschild 1983.
21. Friedman 2013.
22. Ibid., 8.
23. See also Zerubavel 1995; McLuhan and Puddephatt 2019, 85.
24. Zerubavel 1993 [1991], 185.
25. Zerubavel 2007, 134–35.
26. Simmel 1950 [1908], 164–68.
27. See, for example, Zerubavel 1997, 81–99.
28. See, for example, Zerubavel 2003, 48, 84, 103.
29. Glaser and Strauss 1967, 92–93; Zerubavel 1995, 1096.
30. Glaser and Strauss 1967, 155. See also Kuran 1995, xi.
31. Patterson 1982.
32. Naroll et al. 1974.
33. Zerubavel 2003, 48–52. See also Y. Zerubavel, forthcoming.
34. Zerubavel 1982a; Zerubavel 1985 [1981], 82–95.
35. Zerubavel, forthcoming.
36. Simmel 1955 [1908], 100.
37. Zerubavel 2006, 8.
38. Glaser and Strauss 1967, 81. See also 82–90; Glaser and Strauss 1971, 186.
39. Morrill 1995.
40. Poincaré 1921, 386.
41. Vaughan 2009, 697.

42. See Fine 2012, 7–15.
43. Adut 2008.
44. Adut 2018, xi. Emphasis added.
45. Roth 1963; Abbott 1988; Ryan 2006, 235; McLean 2017, 79–84.
46. Zerubavel 1993 [1991], 34, 38–41, 44, 53–54, 58.
47. See, for example, Zerubavel 2006, 6–8, 30.
48. Ibid., 68.
49. Zerubavel 2018, 10.
50. See, for example, Nippert-Eng 1992; Foster 2000; Brekhus 2003; Watson 2005; Spitzer 2006; Germana 2012; Campion 2019; Peña-Alves 2019.
51. Purcell 2001.
52. Mullaney 2006, 190.
53. See, for example, ibid., 188–89. See also Mullaney 2019.
54. DeGloma 2014.
55. Simmel 1950 [1908], 145–69.
56. Zerubavel 1993 [1991], 41.
57. Zerubavel 2003.
58. Zerubavel 2006.
59. Zerubavel 2011, 46–52.

## Chapter 4

1. Snow et al. 2003, 194. Emphasis added.
2. Comte 1975 [1830–42], 244–47. See also Ragin 1987.
3. Weber 1978 [1925], 541–56.
4. See also Brekhus 2007, 458–59.
5. https://www.merriam-webster.com/dictionary/compare.
6. Glaser and Strauss 1971, 186.
7. See, for example, Zerubavel 1993 [1991], 69. See also Jaffe-Dax 2018.
8. See also Schwalbe et al. 2000, 421.
9. See also Comte 1975 [1830–42], 246–47.
10. Zerubavel 2011, 85–86.
11. Coser 1971, 180.
12. See also Prus 1996, 164; Snow et al. 2003, 194; Brekhus 2007, 457.
13. See also Prus 1987, 263, 286; Holyoak and Thagard 1995, 5, 116, 119; Prus 1996, 164.
14. Hochschild 1983, 16. Emphasis added.
15. Bonilla-Silva 2015, 80.

16. Zerubavel 2003, 10.
17. Ibid. Emphases added.
18. Holyoak and Thagard 1995, 39. See also Vaughan 1992, 19.
19. Bartha 2010, 1.
20. Vaughan 2002, 30. See also Vaughan 2004, 315; Vaughan 2014, 61.
21. Zerubavel 2007, 137.
22. Hofstadter and Sander 2013, 3.
23. See also Poincaré 1921, 375.
24. Simmel 1959 [1908], 316–17. Emphasis added.
25. Simmel 1897–98, 663. Emphasis added.
26. Vaughan 2002, 30. Emphasis added.
27. Vaughan 2009, 697.
28. Vaughan 1998, 7.
29. Coser 1994, 1. Emphasis added.
30. Hughes 1971 [1945].
31. Goffman 1961, 4–5.
32. Goffman 1963.
33. Zerubavel 1993 [1991], 6–10, 14.
34. Zerubavel 2015, 56–57.
35. Zerubavel 2018, 12.
36. Ibid., 95–96.
37. On the mental acts of lumping and splitting, see also Zerubavel 1993 [1991], 16–17, 21; Zerubavel 1996; Zerubavel 2003, 80, 98.
38. On foregrounding and backgrounding, see Zerubavel 2006, 65–68; Zerubavel 2015, 45–46, 82–89; Zerubavel 2018, 60–91.
39. See also Francis 2015, 15.
40. See also Friedman 2013.
41. Zerubavel 1993 [1991], 79.
42. Zerubavel 1997, 45–47, 39–40, 51–52.
43. Zerubavel 2015, 59.
44. Spencer 1969 [1876], 36.
45. Durkheim 1984 [1893], 35–37, 48–52.
46. Eliade 1959 [1949]; van Gennep 1960 [1909]; Mauss 1967 [1925].
47. Dubnov 2016.
48. Tavory and Winchester 2012.
49. Martin 2009, 206, 255–56.
50. Zerubavel 1989 [1985], 28–43.
51. Zerubavel 1993 [1991], 52–55.
52. Zerubavel 2003, 9.

53. Ibid., 105–09.
54. Brooke 1998.
55. Ibid.
56. Dowd 1998.
57. Zerubavel 2003, 38.
58. Ibid., 91.
59. Ibid., 52.
60. Ibid., 47.
61. Ibid., 31. See also 32–33.
62. Ibid., 83–85, 90.
63. Ibid., 84.
64. On the extra-academic, *political* use of historical analogies, see also ibid., 48–52; Y. Zerubavel, forthcoming.
65. Burke 1984 [1935], 89.
66. Skocpol 1979.
67. Weyland 2012, 918.
68. Whitehead 2011, Springborg 2011; Weyland 2012.
69. Coser 1974, 11–13, 21–31.
70. Zerubavel 2003, 39.
71. Zerubavel 2011, 124–25.
72. Swidler 1986.
73. Zerubavel 1993 [1991], 56–57.
74. Holland et al. 1986, 289. See also Hofstadter and Sander 2013, 17; Vaughan 2014, 61.
75. Brubaker 2016, ix. Emphasis added.
76. Ibid., 9.
77. Simmel 1959 [1908], 316–17.
78. Van Gennep 1960 [1909], 15–25.
79. Ibid., 50–64, 146–65.
80. Ibid., 3. Emphasis added.
81. Ibid., 26–40, 65–145.
82. Barthes 1968 [1964], 25–30. See also Saussure 1959 [1915], 16–17.
83. Zerubavel 2018, 2.
84. Birdwhistell 1970.
85. Lévi-Strauss 1967 [1958], 32. Emphases added. See also 207–09.
86. Pike 1967 [1954], 73–118.
87. Leach 1964. See also Zerubavel 1993 [1991], 39–41.
88. Blau 1977, 47.
89. Moody and White 2003.

90. Coser 1971, 180.
91. Chase 1991, 134.
92. Vaughan 2002.
93. Chancer 1992.
94. Ebaugh 1988.
95. Rothman 2016, 12, 56, 178.
96. Reysen and Branscombe 2010. See also Campion 2019.
97. Ponticelli 1999. See also Berger 1963, 58–65; DeGloma 2014.
98. Zerubavel 1993 [1991], 72.
99. Ibid., 24.
100. Ibid., 43. See also DiMaggio 1982.
101. Zerubavel 1993 [1991], 7–9.
102. Ibid., 33–60, 115–22.
103. Zerubavel 2015, 74.
104. Ibid., 62–63.
105. Ibid., 28–31, 35.
106. Ibid., 46–48.
107. Ibid., 67–68.
108. Ibid., 60.
109. Zerubavel 2003, 42.
110. Zerubavel 2006, 50–51.
111. Zerubavel 2011, 16–21, 55.
112. Ibid., 118–22, 126.
113. Ibid., 95–97.
114. Ibid., 127–29.
115. Zerubavel 2018. On the formal parallels between straightness and able-bodiedness, see also McRuer 2006.
116. Zerubavel 2018, 63–85.
117. Ibid., 86.
118. Ibid., 93.
119. Ibid., 67–68.
120. See, for example, Benedict 2005 [1934]; Mead 1935.
121. See, for example, Purcell 2001; Watson 2005; Mullaney 2006; Campion 2019.
122. DeGloma and Papadantonakis 2020.
123. DeGloma (n.d.).
124. Brekhus 2003, 140–43.
125. Spitzer 2006.
126. Foster 2000.

127. Nippert-Eng 1992.
128. Germana 2012.
129. Howard 2006; Howard 2008a.
130. Howard 2006, 308, 310.
131. Howard 2008b, 9–10. Emphases added.
132. Lizardo and Pirkey 2014, 37. See also Blau 1964.
133. Kadushin 2012, 18–21.
134. Rivera 2008.
135. Y. Zerubavel 2019. See especially 216–28.
136. Peña-Alves 2019.
137. Zerubavel 2006.
138. Zerubavel 2011, 31–52.
139. Ibid., 12.
140. Zerubavel 1993 [1991], 18–20.
141. Zerubavel 2003, 9.
142. Tracy 1981.

# Chapter 5

1. See, for example, Zerubavel 1977; Zerubavel 1979, xix–xx, 9–34, 46–83, 88–104, 124–30; Zerubavel 1985 [1981], 31–40, 70–100; Zerubavel 1982a; Zerubavel 1982b; Zerubavel 1989 [1985], 5–82; Zerubavel 1992.
2. Zerubavel 1993 [1991], 116; Zerubavel 2015, 74–75.
3. Zerubavel 1993 [1991], 116, 158n2.
4. Pirsig 1981 [1974], 70. See also 66.
5. Brekhus 2007, 458.
6. See, for example, Jaffe-Dax 2018. See also Zerubavel 1993 [1991], 69.
7. Spender 1980, 165. See also Haaken 1988, 312.
8. See also Gould 2003, 13.
9. McLuhan and Puddephatt 2019, 72.
10. See also Geertz 1973, 22; Zerubavel 1979, xvii; Zerubavel 1985 [1981], x.
11. See also Davis 1971, 317–18.
12. Evans-Pritchard 1940, 106–08, 200–01.
13. Zerubavel 2011, 31–52.
14. See, for example, Koestler 1964, 112–14.
15. See also Prus 1987, 263; Prus 1996, 142, 165.
16. Zerubavel 2011, 12, 138n64.
17. Ibid., 12.

18. Zerubavel 2003, 104–09.
19. Ibid., 8–9.
20. Zerubavel 2006, 14.
21. On the difference between *in*attention and *dis*attention, see Zerubavel 2015, 60.
22. See also Lofland and Lofland 1995, 157–59; Jutel 2017, 3, 12.
23. See also Simmel 1950 [1917], 11; Zerubavel 1979, xvii.
24. See also Zerubavel 2018, 33–35, 69–72, 80–84.
25. Brod 2002, 166–67.
26. Burke 1984 [1935], 89.
27. On their extratheoretical, political benefits, see, for example, May 1973; Neustadt and May 1986; Khong 1992; Zerubavel 2003, 48–52; Saguy 2020; Y. Zerubavel, forthcoming.
28. Weber 1978 [1925], 215, 241–45, 1111–56; Berger 1963, 62.
29. Bourdieu 1977 [1972].
30. Garfinkel 1967, 116–85; Saguy 2020, 27–28; Enriquez and Saguy 2016, 109–10. See also García 2019, 133–69.
31. Stryker 2015 (retrieved October 21, 2018). See also Brubaker 2016.
32. Crenshaw 1989.
33. See also Brekhus 1996, 514.
34. Zerubavel 2011, 62–64, 101–03; Zerubavel 2018, 13.
35. Brekhus 1996, 514.
36. Ibid., 515–16. See also Mullaney 1999, 269.
37. Zerubavel 2018, 13–14.
38. Kitsuse 1980, 8–9. On victims of sexual assault, see also Saguy 2020, 83–110.
39. Saguy and Ward 2011; Saguy 2020, 30–43.
40. Saguy 2020, 68–82.
41. Enriquez and Saguy 2016; Saguy 2020, 44–67.
42. Saguy 2020, 1–2.
43. Yonan 2013 (retrieved May 15, 2019).
44. Saguy 2020, 2, 83–86, 95–103.
45. Hughes 1971 [1956], 439–40.
46. Prus 1987, 264.
47. Gould 2003, 17–18. Emphasis added.
48. Coser 1971, 179. Emphasis added.
49. Prus 1987, 264. Emphasis added.
50. Zerubavel 2003, 9.

51. On the conventional distinction between "source" and "target" analogs, see, for example, Holyoak and Thagard 1995, 2.
52. See also Glaser and Strauss 1967, 83–84.
53. See also Prus 1987, 264.
54. See also Holyoak and Thagard 1995, 196.
55. Hughes 1971 [1951b], 342.
56. Hughes 1971 [1951a], 316.
57. Zerubavel 2018, 69–72.
58. Zerubavel 1993 [1991], 113. Emphases added.
59. Koestler 1964, 95. Emphasis added. See also 35, 94.
60. Ibid., 94. See also Hadamard 1945, 29.
61. James 1983 [1890], 500.
62. Koestler 1964.
63. Ibid., 105–08.
64. Miller 1978, 187, 207–10.
65. Freud 1918 [1913].
66. See also Emerson 1898 [1837], 87–88; Bronowski 1965 [1956], 15; Holyoak and Thagard 1995, 185–209.
67. Hofstadter and Sander 2013, 509. See also 17; Davis 1971, 315; Kuran 1995, xi; Holyoak and Thagard 1995, 4.
68. Smith 1989, 24.
69. Vaughan 2002, 30.
70. Hofstadter and Sander 2013, 515. Emphases added. See also Bronowski 1965 [1956], 16, 19.
71. Hofstadter and Sander 2013, 17.
72. Ibid., 30. Emphasis added.
73. Emerson 1898 [1836], 49. See also Lévi-Strauss 1978, 8; Holyoak and Thagard 1995, 9.
74. Hofstadter and Sander 2013, 340. See also Holyoak and Thagard 1995, 19.
75. See also Coser 1971, 179.
76. Hofstadter and Sander 2013, 288. Emphasis added.
77. Reed 1848, 504. Emphasis added.
78. See also Zerubavel 2006, 14.

# Bibliography

Abbott, Andrew. *The System of Professions: An Essay on the Division of Expert Labor*. Chicago: University of Chicago Press, 1988.

Adut, Ari. *On Scandal: Moral Disturbances in Society, Politics, and Art*. Cambridge, UK: Cambridge University Press, 2008.

———. *Reign of Appearances: The Misery and Splendor of the Public Sphere*. Cambridge, UK: Cambridge University Press, 2018.

Arendt, Hannah. "Walter Benjamin: 1892–1940." In *Men in Dark Times*, 153–206. San Diego, CA: Harcourt Brace, 1968.

Bartha, Paul F. A. *By Parallel Reasoning: The Construction and Evaluation of Analogical Arguments*. New York: Oxford University Press, 2010.

Barthes, Roland. *Elements of Semiology*. New York: Hill & Wang, 1968 [1964].

Battle, Brittany. "War Widows and Welfare Queens: The Semiotics of Deservingness in the US Welfare System." In Wayne H. Brekhus and Gabe Ignatow (eds.), *The Oxford Handbook of Cognitive Sociology*, 585–605. New York: Oxford University Press, 2019.

Becker, Howard S. *Tricks of the Trade: How to Think About Your Research While You're Doing It*. Chicago: University of Chicago Press, 1998.

Benedict, Ruth. *Patterns of Culture*. Boston: Houghton Mifflin, 2005 [1934].

Berger, Peter L. *Invitation to Sociology: A Humanistic Perspective*. Garden City, NY: Anchor Books, 1963.

Berger, Peter L., and Thomas Luckmann. *The Social Construction of Reality: A Treatise in the Sociology of Knowledge*. Garden City, NY: Doubleday Anchor, 1967 [1966].

Birdwhistell, Ray L. *Kinesics and Context: Essays on Body Motion Communication*. Philadelphia: University of Pennsylvania Press, 1970.

Blau, Peter M. *Exchange and Power in Social Life*. New York: Wiley, 1964.

———. *Inequality and Heterogeneity: A Primitive Theory of Social Structure*. New York: Free Press, 1977.

Blumer, Herbert. "Science Without Concepts." *American Journal of Sociology* 36 (1931): 513–33.

———. "What Is Wrong with Social Theory?" *American Sociological Review* 19 (1954): 3–10.

———. "Sociological Analysis and the 'Variable.'" *American Sociological Review* 21 (1956): 683–90.

——. *Symbolic Interactionism: Perspective and Method*. Englewood Cliffs, NJ: Prentice-Hall, 1969.

Bonilla-Silva, Eduardo. "More Than Prejudice: Restatement, Reflections, and New Directions in Critical Race Theory." *Sociology of Race and Ethnicity* 1 (2015): 75–89.

Bourdieu, Pierre. *Outline of a Theory of Practice*. Cambridge, UK: Cambridge University Press, 1977 [1972].

Brekhus, Wayne H. "Social Marking and the Mental Coloring of Identity: Sexual Identity Construction and Maintenance in the United States." *Sociological Forum* 11 (1996): 497–522.

——. *Peacocks, Chameleons, Centaurs: Gay Suburbia and the Grammar of Social Identity*. Chicago: University of Chicago Press, 2003.

——. "The Rutgers School: A Zerubavelian Culturalist Cognitive Sociology." *European Journal of Social Theory* 10 (2007): 448–64.

Brod, Harry. "Studying Masculinities as Superordinate Studies." In Judith K. Gardiner (ed.), *Masculinity Studies and Feminist Theory: New Directions*, 161–75. New York: Columbia University Press, 2002.

Brodsky, Jodi E. "Intellectual Snobbery: A Socio-Historical Perspective." Unpublished Ph.D. dissertation, Columbia University, 1987.

Bronowski, Jacob. "The Creative Mind." In *Science and Human Values*, 1–24. New York: Harper & Row, 1965 [1956].

Brooke, James. "Conquistador Statue Stirs Hispanic Pride and Indian Rage." *New York Times*, 9 February 1998, sec. A, p. 10.

Brubaker, Rogers. *Trans: Gender and Race in an Age of Unsettled Identities*. Princeton, NJ: Princeton University Press, 2016.

Burawoy, Michael. "The Extended Case Method." *Sociological Theory* 16 (1998): 4–33.

——. *The Extended Case Method: Four Countries, Four Decades, Four Great Transformations, and One Theoretical Tradition*. Berkeley: University of California Press, 2009.

Burke, Kenneth. *Permanence and Change: An Anatomy of Purpose*. 3rd ed. Berkeley: University of California Press, 1984 [1935].

Campion, Lisa. "Doing Identity: A Social Pattern Analysis Exploring the Process of Identity Construction and Maintenance." Unpublished Ph.D. dissertation, Rutgers University, 2019.

Chancer, Lynn S. *Sadomasochism in Everyday Life: The Dynamics of Power and Powerlessness*. New Brunswick, NJ: Rutgers University Press, 1992.

——. *High-Profile Crimes: When Legal Cases Become Social Causes*. Chicago: University of Chicago Press, 2005.

Charmaz, Kathy. *Constructing Grounded Theory*. 2nd ed. Los Angeles: SAGE, 2014.

Chase, Ivan D. "Vacancy Chains." *Annual Review of Sociology* 17 (1991): 133–54.

Chayko, Mary. *Connecting: How We Form Social Bonds and Communities in the Internet Age.* Albany: State University of New York Press, 2002.

Collins, Lynn E. "Intercultural Interpretation of Experience: A Phenomenological Approach." Unpublished Ph.D. dissertation, Columbia University, 1985.

Comte, Auguste. "Cours de Philosophie Positive." In Gertrud Lenzer (ed.), *Auguste Comte and Positivism: The Essential Writings,* 71–306. New York: Harper Torchbooks, 1975 [1830–42].

Coser, Lewis A. *Masters of Sociological Thought: Ideas in Historical and Social Context.* New York: Harcourt Brace Jovanovich, 1971.

———. *Greedy Institutions: Patterns of Undivided Commitment.* New York: Free Press, 1974.

———. "Introduction: Everett Cherrington Hughes 1897–1983." In Everett C. Hughes (ed.), *Work, Race, and the Sociological Imagination,* 1–17. Chicago: University of Chicago Press, 1994.

Crenshaw, Kimberlé. "Demarginalizing the Intersection of Race and Sex: A Black Feminist Critique of Antidiscrimination Doctrine, Feminist Theory and Antiracist Politics." *University of Chicago Legal Forum* 1 (1989): 139–67.

Davenport, Thomas H., and John C. Beck. *The Attention Economy: Understanding the New Currency of Business.* Boston: Harvard Business School Press, 2001.

Davis, Murray S. "That's Interesting! Towards a Phenomenology of Sociology and a Sociology of Phenomenology." *Philosophy of the Social Sciences* 1 (1971): 309–44.

———. "Georg Simmel and Erving Goffman: Legitimators of the Sociological Investigation of Human Experience." *Qualitative Sociology* 20 (1997): 369–88.

DeGloma, Thomas. *Seeing the Light: The Social Logic of Personal Discovery.* Chicago: University of Chicago Press, 2014.

———. *Anonymous: The Performance and Impact of Hidden Identities.* Unpublished book manuscript. n.d.

DeGloma, Thomas, and Max Papadantonakis. "The Thematic Lens: A Formal and Cultural Framework for Comparative Ethnographic Analysis." In Corey M. Abramson and Neil Gong (eds.), *Beyond the Case: Competing Logics and Approaches to Comparative Ethnography,* 84–106. New York: Oxford University Press, 2020.

Denzin, Norman K. *The Research Act: A Theoretical Introduction to Sociological Methods.* Chicago: Aldine, 1970.

DiMaggio, Paul. "Cultural Entrepreneurship in Nineteenth-Century Boston: The Creation of an Organizational Base for High Culture in America." *Media, Culture and Society* 4 (1982): 33–50.

Dowd, Maureen. "Center Holding." *New York Times,* 20 May 1998, sec. A, p. 23.

Dubnov, Arie M. "Notes on the Zionist Passage to India, or: The Analogical Imagination and Its Boundaries." *Journal of Israeli Society* 35 (2016): 177–214.

Durkheim, Emile. *The Division of Labor in Society*. New York: Free Press, 1984 [1893].

———. *The Rules of Sociological Method*. New York: Free Press, 1982 [1895].

———. *The Elementary Forms of Religious Life*. New York: Free Press, 1995 [1912].

———. "The Dualism of Human Nature and Its Social Conditions." In Robert N. Bellah (ed.), *Emile Durkheim: On Morality and Society*, 149–63. Chicago: University of Chicago Press, 1973 [1914].

Dyson, Freeman. *Imagined Worlds*. Cambridge, MA: Harvard University Press, 1997.

Ebaugh, Helen R. F. *Becoming an Ex: The Process of Role Exit*. Chicago: University of Chicago Press, 1988.

Eliade, Mircea. *Cosmos and History: The Myth of the Eternal Return*. New York: Harper Torchbooks, 1959 [1949].

Elkana, Yehuda. *The Discovery of the Conservation of Energy*. Cambridge, MA: Harvard University Press, 1974.

Emerson, Ralph W. "Nature." In *Nature, Addresses, and Lectures*, 13–80. Houghton, Mifflin, and Co., 1898 [1836].

———. "The American Scholar." In *Nature, Addresses, and Lectures*, 83–115. Houghton, Mifflin, and Co., 1898 [1837].

Enriquez, Laura E., and Abigail C. Saguy. "Coming out of the Shadows: Harnessing a Cultural Schema to Advance the Undocumented Immigrant Youth Movement." *American Journal of Cultural Sociology* 4 (2016): 107–30.

Erikson, Emily. "Formalist and Relational Theory in Social Network Analysis." *Sociological Theory* 31 (2013): 219–42.

Erikson, Kai T. *Wayward Puritans: A Study in the Sociology of Deviance*. Boston: Allyn & Bacon, 2005 [1966].

———. *The Sociologist's Eye: Reflections on Social Life*. New Haven, CT: Yale University Press, 2017.

Evans-Pritchard, Edward E. *The Nuer: A Description of the Modes of Livelihood and Political Institutions of a Nilotic People*. London: Oxford University Press, 1940.

Fine, Gary A. *Morel Tales: The Culture of Mushrooming*. Cambridge, MA: Harvard University Press, 1998.

———. *Tiny Publics: Idiocultures and the Power of the Local*. New York: Russell Sage Foundation, 2012.

Fleck, Ludwik. *Genesis and Development of a Scientific Fact*. Chicago: University of Chicago Press, 1979 [1935].

Foster, Johanna. "Feminist Theory and the Politics of Ambiguity: A Comparative Analysis of the Multiracial Movement, the Intersex Movement and the Disability Rights Movement as Contemporary Struggles over Social Classification in the United States." Unpublished Ph.D. dissertation, Rutgers University, 2000.

Francis, Ara. *Family Trouble: Middle-Class Parents, Children's Problems, and the Disruption of Everyday Life.* New Brunswick, NJ: Rutgers University Press, 2015.

Freese, Lee. "Formal Theorizing." *Annual Review of Sociology* 6 (1980): 187–212.

Freud, Sigmund. *Totem and Taboo: Resemblances between the Psychic Lives of Savages and Neurotics.* New York: Vintage Books, 1918 [1913].

Friedman, Asia. *Blind to Sameness: Sexpectations and the Social Construction of Male and Female Bodies.* Chicago: University of Chicago Press, 2013.

García, Angela S. *Legal Passing: Navigating Undocumented Life and Local Immigration Law.* Oakland: University of California Press, 2019.

Garfinkel, Harold. *Studies in Ethnomethodology.* Englewood Cliffs, NJ: Prentice-Hall, 1967.

Geertz, Clifford. "Thick Description: Toward an Interpretive Theory of Culture." In *The Interpretation of Cultures: Selected Essays*, 3–30. New York: Basic Books, 1973.

Germana, Rachelle. "Hyphenation and Its Discontents: Hyphenators, Hyphen-Haters, and the Cultural Politics of Ambiguity." Unpublished Ph.D. dissertation, Rutgers University, 2012.

Glaser, Barney G. *Theoretical Sensitivity.* Mill Valley, CA: The Sociology Press, 1978.

Glaser, Barney G., and Anselm L. Strauss. *The Discovery of Grounded Theory: Strategies for Qualitative Research.* Chicago: Aldine, 1967.

———. *Status Passage: A Formal Theory.* Chicago: Aldine & Atherton, 1971.

Goffman, Erving. "On the Characteristics of Total Institutions." In *Asylums: Essays on the Social Situation of Mental Patients and Other Inmates*, 3–124. Garden City, NY: Doubleday Anchor, 1961.

———. *Stigma: Notes on the Management of Spoiled Identity.* Englewood Cliffs, NJ: Prentice-Hall, 1963.

Gould, Roger V. *Collision of Wills: How Ambiguity about Social Rank Breeds Conflict.* Chicago: University of Chicago Press, 2003.

Greenwald, David S., and Steven J. Zeitlin. *No Reason to Talk About It: Families Confront the Nuclear Taboo.* New York: Norton, 1987.

Gricar, Julie M. "How Thick Is Blood? The Social Construction and Cultural Configuration of Kinship." Unpublished Ph.D. dissertation, Columbia University, 1991.

Haaken, Janice. "Field Dependence Research: A Historical Analysis of a Psychological Construct." *Signs* 13 (1988): 311–30.

Hadamard, Jacques. *An Essay on the Psychology of Invention in the Mathematical Field.* Princeton, NJ: Princeton University Press, 1945.

Hanemaayer, Ariane. "A Grounded Theory Approach to Engaging Technology on the Paintball Field." In Phillip Vannini (ed.), *Material Culture and Technology in Everyday Life*, 157–68. New York: Lang, 2009.

Hochschild, Arlie. *The Managed Heart: Commercialization of Human Feeling.* Berkeley: University of California Press, 1983.

Hofstadter, Douglas, and Emmanuel Sander. *Surfaces and Essences: Analogy as the Fuel and Fire of Thinking.* New York: Basic Books, 2013.

Holland, John, et al. *Induction: Processes of Inference, Learning, and Discovery.* Cambridge, MA: MIT Press, 1986.

Holyoak, Keith J., and Paul Thagard. *Mental Leaps: Analogy in Creative Thought.* Cambridge, MA: MIT Press, 1995.

Horwitz, Allan V. *The Logic of Social Control.* New York: Plenum, 1990.

Howard, Jenna. "Expecting and Accepting: The Temporal Ambiguity of Recovery Identities." *Social Psychology Quarterly* 69 (2006): 307–24.

——. "Negotiating an Exit: Existential, Interactional, and Cultural Obstacles to Disorder Disidentification." *Social Psychology Quarterly* 71 (2008a): 177–92.

——. "Recovering from Recovery: The Temporal Management of Disorder Identity Careers." Unpublished Ph.D. dissertation, Rutgers University, 2008b.

Hughes, Everett C. "Dilemmas and Contradictions of Status." In *The Sociological Eye: Selected Papers*, 141–50. Chicago: Aldine & Atherton, 1971 [1945].

——. "Mistakes at Work." In *The Sociological Eye: Selected Papers*, 316–25. Chicago: Aldine & Atherton, 1971 [1951a].

——. "Work and Self." In *The Sociological Eye: Selected Papers*, 338–47. Chicago: Aldine & Atherton, 1971 [1951b].

——. "The Improper Study of Man." In *The Sociological Eye: Selected Papers*, 431–42. Chicago: Aldine & Atherton. 1971 [1956].

Isaacson, Nicole. "'The Unfinished Infant': An Analysis of the Cultural Representations and Practices to Finish the Premature Baby." Unpublished Ph.D. dissertation, Rutgers University, 2001.

Jaffe-Dax, Tali. "How Can You Even Compare?! The Socio-Cognitive 'Propriety' and 'Deviance' of Analogies." Unpublished paper, Rutgers University, 2018.

James, William. *The Principles of Psychology.* Cambridge, MA: Harvard University Press, 1983 [1890].

Jordan, Mark. *The Silence of Sodom: Homosexuality in Modern Catholicism.* Chicago: University of Chicago Press, 2000.

Jutel, Annemarie. "Beyond the Sociology of Diagnosis." *Sociology Compass* 9 (2015): 841–52.

———. "'The Expertness of His Healer': Diagnosis, Disclosure, and the Power of a Profession." *Health: An Interdisciplinary Journal for the Social Study of Health, Illness, and Medicine*, December 12, 2017, 1–17.

———. *Diagnosis: Truths and Tales*. Toronto, Canada: University of Toronto Press, 2019.

Kadushin, Charles. *Understanding Social Networks: Theories, Concepts, and Findings*. New York: Oxford University Press, 2012.

Kantorovich, Aharon. *Scientific Discovery: Logic and Tinkering*. Albany: State University of New York Press, 1993.

Kennedy, Mary M. "Generalizing from Single-Case Studies." *Evaluation Quarterly* 3 (1979): 661–78.

Khong, Yuen F. *Analogies at War: Korea, Munich, Dien Bien Phu, and the Vietnam Decisions of 1965*. Princeton, NJ: Princeton University Press, 1992.

Kidahashi, Miwako. "Dual Organization: A Study of a Japanese-Owned Firm in the United States." Unpublished Ph.D. dissertation, Columbia University, 1987.

Kitsuse, John I. "Coming out All over: Deviants and the Politics of Social Problems." *Social Problems* 28 (1980): 1–13.

Koestler, Arthur. *The Act of Creation*. London: Hutchinson, 1964.

Koningsveld, Herman. *Empirical Laws, Regularity, and Necessity*. Wageningen, the Netherlands: H. Veenman & Zonen, 1973.

Kuhn, Thomas S. *The Structure of Scientific Revolutions*. 2nd enlarged ed. Chicago: University of Chicago Press, 1970 [1962].

Kuran, Timur. *Private Truths, Public Lies: The Social Consequences of Preference Falsification*. Cambridge, MA: Harvard University Press, 1995.

Leach, Edmund. "Anthropological Aspects of Language: Animal Categories and Verbal Abuse." In Eric H. Lenneberg (ed.), *New Directions in the Study of Language*, 23–63. Cambridge, MA: MIT Press, 1964.

Levine, Donald N. "The Structure of Simmel's Social Thought." In Kurt H. Wolff (ed.), *Georg Simmel, 1858–1918*, 9–32. Columbus: Ohio State University Press, 1959.

Lévi-Strauss, Claude. *Structural Anthropology*. Garden City, NY: Anchor Books, 1967 [1958].

———. *Myth and Meaning*. Toronto, Canada: University of Toronto Press, 1978.

Lizardo, Omar, and Melissa F. Pirkey. "How Organizational Theory Can Help Network Theorizing: Linking Structure and Dynamics via Cross-Level Analogies." *Research in the Sociology of Organizations* 40 (2014): 33–56.

Lofland, John. *Doing Social Life: The Qualitative Study of Human Interaction in Natural Settings*. New York: Wiley, 1976.

———. "Analytic Ethnography: Features, Failings, and Futures." *Journal of Contemporary Ethnography* 24 (1995): 30–67.

Lofland, John, and Lyn H. Lofland. *Analyzing Social Settings: A Guide to Qualitative Observation and Analysis*. 3rd ed. Belmont, CA: Wadsworth, 1995.

Malyk, Maria V. "Sincere Backhanded Compliments: Exploring Social, Semiotic, and Cognitive Dimensions of Cryptosemic Interaction." Unpublished Ph.D. dissertation, Rutgers University, 2014.

Margalit, Avishai. *The Ethics of Memory*. Cambridge, MA: Harvard University Press, 2002.

Martin, John L. *Social Structures*. Princeton, NJ: Princeton University Press, 2009.

Mauss, Marcel. *The Gift: Forms and Functions of Exchange in Archaic Societies*. New York: Norton, 1967 [1925].

May, Ernest R. *"Lessons" of the Past: The Use and Misuse of History in American Foreign Policy*. New York: Oxford University Press, 1973.

McLean, Paul. *Culture in Networks*. Cambridge, UK: Polity Press, 2017.

McLuhan, Arthur, and Antony Puddephatt. "Overcoming 'Analytic Interruptus': The Genesis, Development, and Future of Generic Social Processes." In Norman K. Denzin (ed.), *The Interaction Order*, 71–93. Bingley, UK: Emerald Publishing, 2019.

McRuer, Robert. *Crip Theory: Cultural Signs of Queerness and Disability*. New York: New York University Press, 2006.

Mead, George H. *Mind, Self, and Society*. Chicago: University of Chicago Press, 1934.

Mead, Margaret. *Sex and Temperament in Three Primitive Societies*. New York: Morrow, 1935.

Merton, Robert K. "Socially Expected Durations: A Case Study of Concept Formation in Sociology." In Walter W. Powell and Richard Robbins (eds.), *Conflict and Consensus: A Festschrift in Honor of Lewis A. Coser*, 262–83. New York: Free Press, 1984.

Meyer, Jan H. F., et al. (eds.). *Threshold Concepts and Transformational Learning*. Rotterdam, the Netherlands: Sense Publishers, 2010.

Miller, Jonathan. *The Body in Question*. New York: Random House, 1978.

Mills, C. Wright. *The Sociological Imagination*. New York: Oxford University Press, 1959.

Moody, James, and Douglas R. White. "Structural Cohesion and Embeddedness: A Hierarchical Concept of Social Groups." *American Sociological Review* 68 (2003): 103–27.

Morrill, Calvin. *The Executive Way: Conflict Management in Corporations*. Chicago: University of Chicago Press, 1995.

Mullaney, Jamie L. "Making It 'Count': Mental Weighing and Identity Attribution." *Symbolic Interaction* 22 (1999): 269–83.

———. *Everyone Is NOT Doing It: Abstinence and Personal Identity*. Chicago: University of Chicago Press, 2006.

———. "Social Mindscapes and the Self: The Case for Social Pattern Analysis." In Wayne H. Brekhus and Gabe Ignatow (eds.), *The Oxford Handbook of Cognitive Sociology*, 388–402. New York: Oxford University Press, 2019.

Naroll, Raoul, et al. *Military Deterrence in History: A Pilot Cross-Historical Survey*. Albany: State University of New York Press, 1974.

Neisser, Ulric. "Visual Research." *Scientific American* 210 (June 1964): 94.

Neustadt, Richard E., and Ernest R. May. *Thinking in Time: The Uses of History for Decision-Makers*. New York: Free Press, 1986.

Nippert-Eng, Christena E. "'Mommy, Mommy,' or 'Excuse Me, Ma'am': Gender and Interruptions at Home and Work." Paper presented at the annual meeting of the American Sociological Association, Pittsburgh, PA, August 1992.

———. *Home and Work: Negotiating Boundaries through Everyday Life*. Chicago: University of Chicago Press, 1996.

———. *Watching Closely: A Guide to Ethnographic Observation*. New York: Oxford University Press, 2015.

Parsons, Talcott. *The Social System*. New York: Free Press, 1951.

Patterson, Orlando. *Slavery and Social Death: A Comparative Study*. Cambridge, MA: Harvard University Press, 1982.

Pearce, Richard M. "Chance and the Prepared Mind." *Science New Series* 35.912 (June 21, 1912): 941–56.

Peña-Alves, Stephanie. "Marked Passages: A Formal Analysis of Boundary Crossings at the Thresholds of the Body, the Home, and the State." Paper presented at the Qualitative Analysis Conference, New Brunswick, Canada, May 2019.

Pike, Kenneth L. *Language in Relation to a Unified Theory of the Structure of Human Behavior*. The Hague, the Netherlands: Mouton, 1967 [1954].

Pirsig, Robert M. *Zen and the Art of Motorcycle Maintenance*. New York: Bantam New Age, 1981 [1974].

Poincaré, Henri. *The Foundations of Science*. New York: Science Press, 1921.

Pollock, Mica. *Colormute: Race Talk Dilemmas in an American School*. Princeton, NJ: Princeton University Press, 2004.

Ponticelli, Christy M. "Crafting Stories of Sexual Identity Reconstruction." *Social Psychology Quarterly* 62 (1999): 157–72.

Proust, Marcel. *Remembrance of Things Past, Vol. 2*. Hertfordshire, UK: Wordworth Editions, 2006 [1923].

Prus, Robert. "Generic Social Processes: Maximizing Conceptual Development in Ethnographic Research." *Journal of Contemporary Ethnography* 16 (1987): 250–93.

———. *Symbolic Interaction and Ethnographic Research: Intersubjectivity and the Study of Human Lived Experience*. Albany: State University of New York Press, 1996.

———. "Ethnographic Comparisons, Complexities and Conceptualities: Generic Social Processes and the Pragmatic Accomplishment of Group Life." *Comparative Sociology* 9 (2010): 496–527.

Puddephatt, Antony, and Arthur McLuhan. "Generic Social Processes: Reimagining a Conceptual Schema for Grounded Theory in the Contemporary Era." *Sociological Focus* 52 (2019): 140–55.

Purcell, Kristen. "Leveling the Playing Field: Constructing Parity in the Modern World." Unpublished Ph.D. dissertation, Rutgers University, 2001.

Ragin, Charles C. *The Comparative Method: Moving Beyond Qualitative and Quantitative Strategies*. Berkeley: University of California Press. 1987.

Reed, Henry (ed.). *The Complete Poetical Works of William Wordsworth*. Pittsburgh, PA: Kay & Troutman, 1848.

Reysen, Stephen, and Nyla R. Branscombe. "Fanship and Fandom: Comparisons Between Sport and Non-Sport Fans." *Journal of Sport Behavior* 33 (2010): 176–93.

Rivera, Lauren A. "Managing 'Spoiled' National Identity: War, Tourism, and Memory in Croatia." *American Sociological Review* 73 (2008): 613–34.

Rivera, Mark T., et al. "Dynamics of Dyads in Social Networks: Assortative, Relational, and Proximity Mechanisms." *Annual Review of Sociology* 36 (2010): 91–115.

Roth, Julius A. *Timetables: Structuring the Passage of Time in Hospital Treatment and Other Careers*. Indianapolis, IN: Bobbs-Merrill, 1963.

Rothman, Barbara K. *A Bun in the Oven: How the Food and Birth Movements Resist Industrialization*. New York: New York University Press, 2016.

Ryan, Dan. "Getting the Word out: Notes on the Social Organization of Notification." *Sociological Theory* 24 (2006): 228–54.

Saeki, Eiko. "Contested Boundaries of Personhood: The Moral Status of the Fetus and the Infant in Japan, 1750–1886." Unpublished Ph.D. dissertation, Rutgers University, 2017.

Saguy, Abigail C. *Come out, Come out, Whoever You Are*. New York: Oxford University Press, 2020.

Saguy, Abigail C., and Anna Ward. "Coming out as Fat: Rethinking Stigma." *Social Psychology Quarterly* 74 (2011): 53–75.

Saussure, Ferdinand de. *Course in General Linguistics*. New York: Philosophical Library, 1959 [1915].

Schofield, Janet W. "Increasing the Generalizability of Qualitative Research." In Elliott W. Eisner and Alan Peshkin (eds.), *Qualitative Inquiry in Education: The Continuing Debate*, 201–32. New York: Teachers College Press, 1990.

Schutz, Alfred, and Thomas Luckmann. *The Structures of the Life-World*. Evanston, IL: Northwestern University Press, 1973.

Schwalbe, Michael, et al. "Generic Processes in the Reproduction of Inequality: An Interactionist Analysis." *Social Forces* 79 (2000): 419–52.

Schwartz, Howard, and Jerry Jacobs. *Qualitative Sociology: A Method to the Madness.* New York: Free Press, 1979.

Simmel, Georg. "The Persistence of Social Groups." *American Journal of Sociology* 3 (1897–98): 662–75.

———. "Quantitative Aspects of the Group." In Kurt H. Wolff (ed.), *The Sociology of Georg Simmel*, 87–177. New York: Free Press, 1950 [1908].

———. "Conflict." In *Conflict and the Web of Group Affiliations*, 13–123. New York: Free Press, 1955 [1908].

———. "The Problem of Sociology." In Kurt H. Wolff (ed.), *Georg Simmel, 1858–1918: A Collection of Essays with Translations and Bibliography*, 310–35. Columbus: Ohio State University Press, 1959 [1908].

———. "The Field of Sociology." In Kurt H. Wolff (ed.), *The Sociology of Georg Simmel*, 3–25. New York: Free Press, 1950 [1917].

Simpson, Ruth. "The Germ Culture: Modernity, Metaphor, and Epidemic Disease." Unpublished Ph.D. dissertation, Rutgers University, 2006.

Skocpol, Theda. *States and Social Revolutions: A Comparative Analysis of France, Russia, and China.* Cambridge, UK: Cambridge University Press, 1979.

Smith, Gregory W. H. "Snapshots 'Sub Specie Aeternitatis': Simmel, Goffman and Formal Sociology." *Human Studies* 12 (1989): 19–57.

Snow, David A., et al. "Elaborating Analytic Ethnography: Linking Fieldwork and Theory." *Ethnography* 4 (2003): 181–200.

Sorokin, Pitirim A. *Sociocultural Causality, Space, Time: A Study of Referential Principles of Sociology and Social Science.* Durham, NC: Duke University Press, 1943.

Spencer, Herbert. *Principles of Sociology.* Hamden, CT: Archon Books, 1969 [1876].

Spender, Dale. *Man Made Language.* London: Routledge & Kegan Paul, 1980.

Spitzer, Samantha. "Remission: 'Dormant Danger' and 'Liminal Living.'" Paper presented at the annual meeting of the Eastern Sociological Society, Boston, February 2006.

Springborg, Robert. "Whither the Arab Spring? 1989 or 1848?" *The International Spectator* 46.3 (2011): 5–12.

Stein, Karen. *Getting Away from It All: Vacations and Identity.* Philadelphia: Temple University Press, 2019.

Stryker, Susan. "Caitlyn Jenner and Rachel Dolezal: Identification, Embodiment, and Bodily Transformation." July 13, 2015. https://www.historians.org/publications-and-directories/perspectives-on-history/summer-2015/caitlyn-jenner-and-rachel-dolezal-identification-embodiment-and-bodily-transformation (accessed on March 11, 2020).

Swedberg, Richard. "Theorizing in Sociological Research: A New Perspective, a New Departure?" *Annual Review of Sociology* 43 (2017): 189–206.

Swidler, Ann. "Culture in Action: Symbols and Strategies." *American Sociological Review* 51 (1986): 273–86.

Tavory, Iddo, and Stefan Timmermans. *Abductive Analysis: Theorizing Qualitative Research*. Chicago: University of Chicago Press, 2014.

Tavory, Iddo, and Daniel Winchester. "Experiential Careers: The Routinization and De-Routinization of Religious Life." *Theory and Society* 41 (2012): 351–73.

Tracy, David. *The Analogical Imagination: Christian Theology and the Culture of Pluralism*. New York: Crossroad, 1981.

Van den Hoonaard, Will C. *Working with Sensitizing Concepts: Analytical Field Research*. Thousand Oaks, CA: Sage, 1996.

Van Gennep, Arnold. *The Rites of Passage*. Chicago: University of Chicago Press, 1960 [1909].

Vaughan, Diane. "Theory Elaboration: The Heuristics of Case Analysis." In Charles C. Ragin and Howard S. Becker (eds.), *What Is a Case? Exploring the Foundations of Social Inquiry*, 173–202. Cambridge, UK: Cambridge University Press, 1992.

———. "How Theory Travels: Analogy, Models, and the Diffusion of Ideas." Paper presented at the annual meeting of the American Sociological Association, San Francisco, August 1998.

———. "Signals and Interpretive Work: The Role of Culture in a Theory of Practical Action." In Karen A. Cerulo (ed.), *Culture in Mind: Toward a Sociology of Culture and Cognition*, 28–54. New York: Routledge, 2002.

———. "Theorizing Disaster: Analogy, Historical Ethnography, and the Challenger Accident." *Ethnography* 5 (2004): 315–47.

———. "Analytic Ethnography." In Peter Hedström and Peter Bearman (eds.), *The Oxford Handbook of Analytical Sociology*, 688–711. New York: Oxford University Press, 2009.

———. "Analogy, Cases, and Comparative Social Organization." In Richard Swedberg (ed.), *Theorizing in Social Science: The Context of Discovery*, 61–84. Stanford, CA: Stanford University Press, 2014.

Verhoeven, Jef C. "An Interview with Erving Goffman, 1980." *Research on Language and Social Interaction* 26 (1993): 317–48.

Wagner-Pacifici, Robin. *Theorizing the Standoff: Contingency in Action*. Cambridge, UK: Cambridge University Press, 2000.

Wajnryb, Ruth. *The Silence: How Tragedy Shapes Talk*. Crows Nest, Australia: Allen & Unwin, 2001.

Watson, Ian. "Cognitive Design: Creating the Sets of Categories and Labels that Structure Our Shared Experience." Unpublished Ph.D. dissertation, Rutgers University, 2005.

Weber, Max. *The Protestant Ethic and the Spirit of Capitalism*. New York: Viking Penguin, 2002 [1904].

———. *The Methodology of the Social Sciences*. New York: Free Press, 1949 [1903–17].

———. *Economy and Society: An Outline of Interpretive Sociology*. Berkeley: University of California Press, 1978 [1925].

Weyland, Kurt. "The Arab Spring: Why the Surprising Similarities with the Revolutionary Wave of 1848?" *Perspectives on Politics* 10 (2012): 917–34.

Whitehead, Andrew. "Eric Hobsbawm on 2011: 'It Reminds Me of 1848 . . .'" *BBC News Magazine*, December 23, 2011. https://www.bbc.com/news/magazine-16217726 (accessed on July 5, 2019).

Wolfe, Deborah. "Beauty as a Vocation: Women and Beauty Contests in America." Unpublished Ph.D. dissertation, Columbia University, 1994.

Yeh, Hsin-Yi. "The Construction of Identification with Mnemonic Engineering: Toward a Conceptual Framework of Identity-Remembering." *Identity* 18 (2018): 218–31.

Yonan, Joe. "A Former Omnivore Comes out as Vegetarian." *The Washington Post*. March 5, 2013. https://www.washingtonpost.com/lifestyle/food/a-former-omnivore-comes-out-as-vegetarian/2013/03/04/4868316a-8054-11e2-8074-b26a871b165a_story.html (accessed on May 15, 2019).

Zerubavel, Eviatar. "Timetables and Scheduling: On the Social Organization of Time." *Sociological Inquiry* 46 (1976): 87–94.

———. "The French Republican Calendar: A Case Study in the Sociology of Time." *American Sociological Review* 42 (1977): 868–77.

———. *Patterns of Time in Hospital Life: A Sociological Perspective*. Chicago: University of Chicago Press, 1979.

———. "If Simmel Were a Fieldworker: On Formal Sociological Theory and Analytical Field Research." *Symbolic Interaction* 3.2 (1980): 25–33.

———. *Hidden Rhythms: Schedules and Calendars in Social Life*. Berkeley: University of California Press, 1985 [1981].

———. "Easter and Passover: On Calendars and Group Identity." *American Sociological Review* 47 (1982a): 284–89.

———. "The Standardization of Time: A Sociohistorical Perspective." *American Journal of Sociology* 88 (1982b): 1–23.

———. *The Seven-Day Circle: The History and Meaning of the Week*. Chicago: University of Chicago Press, 1989 [1985].

———. *The Fine Line: Making Distinctions in Everyday Life*. Chicago: University of Chicago Press, 1993 [1991].

———. *Terra Cognita: The Mental Discovery of America*. New Brunswick, NJ: Rutgers University Press, 1992.

———. "The Rigid, the Fuzzy, and the Flexible: Notes on the Mental Sculpting of Academic Identity." *Social Research* 62 (1995): 1093–106.

———. "Lumping and Splitting: Notes on Social Classification." *Sociological Forum* 11 (1996): 421–33.

———. *Social Mindscapes: An Invitation to Cognitive Sociology*. Cambridge, MA: Harvard University Press, 1997.

————. *Time Maps: Collective Memory and the Social Shape of the Past.* Chicago: University of Chicago Press, 2003.

————. *The Elephant in the Room: Silence and Denial in Everyday Life.* New York: Oxford University Press, 2006.

————. "Generally Speaking: The Logic and Mechanics of Social Pattern Analysis." *Sociological Forum* 22 (2007): 131–45.

————. *Ancestors and Relatives: Genealogy, Identity, and Community.* New York: Oxford University Press, 2011.

————. *Hidden in Plain Sight: The Social Structure of Irrelevance.* New York: Oxford University Press, 2015.

————. "The Five Pillars of Essentialism: Reification and the Social Construction of an Objective Reality." *Cultural Sociology* 10 (2016): 69–76.

————. *Taken for Granted: The Remarkable Power of the Unremarkable.* Princeton, NJ: Princeton University Press, 2018.

————. "Cognitive Sociology: Between the Personal and the Universal Mind." In Wayne H. Brekhus and Gabe Ignatow (eds.), *The Oxford Handbook of Cognitive Sociology*, 31–41. New York: Oxford University Press, 2019.

————. "The Sociology of Time." In Juliane Reinecke et al. (eds.), *About Time: Temporality and History in Organization Studies.* Oxford: Oxford University Press, forthcoming.

Zerubavel, Yael. *Desert in the Promised Land.* Stanford, CA: Stanford University Press, 2019.

————. "Linearity and Its Disruptions: Event Boundaries, Commemorative Time, and Historical Analogies." *Journal of Israeli History* (forthcoming).

# Author Index

Abbott, Andrew, 32, 79
Adut, Ari, 32, 79
Arendt, Hannah, 75

Bartha, Paul F. A., 80
Barthes, Roland, 50, 81
Battle, Brittany, 75
Beck, John C., 74
Becker, Howard S., 77
Benedict, Ruth, 82
Berger, Peter L., 8, 14, 65, 74, 75,
    76, 82, 84
Birdwhistell, Ray L., 50, 81
Blau, Peter M., 51, 81, 83
Blumer, Herbert, 2–3, 15–16, 73, 76
Bonilla-Silva, Eduardo, 39, 79
Bourdieu, Pierre, 65, 84
Branscombe, Nyla R., 51, 82
Brekhus, Wayne H., 23, 37, 56, 60, 66,
    73, 75, 77, 78, 79, 82, 83, 84
Brod, Harry, 84
Brodsky, Jodi E., 75
Bronowski, Jacob, 85
Brooke, James, 81
Brubaker, Rogers, 49, 81, 84
Burawoy, Michael, 2, 73, 78
Burke, Kenneth, 81, 84

Campion, Lisa, 75, 79, 82
Chancer, Lynn S., 24, 51, 78, 82
Charmaz, Kathy, 73, 74
Chase, Ivan D., 51, 82
Chayko, Mary, 75
Collins, Lynn E., 75
Comte, Auguste, 37, 79

Coser, Lewis A., 13, 17, 48, 51, 68, 76,
    77, 79, 80, 81, 82, 84, 85
Crenshaw, Kimberlé, 84

Davenport, Thomas H., 74
Davis, Murray S., 76, 83, 85
DeGloma, Thomas, 34, 55, 73, 75,
    77, 79, 82
Denzin, Norman K., 73, 77
DiMaggio, Paul, 82
Dowd, Maureen, 45, 81
Dubnov, Arie M., 44, 80
Durkheim, Emile, 1, 10, 13, 34, 44,
    73, 75, 76, 80
Dyson, Freeman, 73

Ebaugh, Helen R. F., 51, 82
Eliade, Mircea, 44, 80
Elkana, Yehuda, 73
Emerson, Ralph W., 72, 85
Enriquez, Laura E., 65, 67, 84
Erikson, Emily, 76
Erikson, Kai T., 15, 18, 76
Evans-Pritchard, Edward E., 61, 83

Fine, Gary A., 32, 73, 79
Fleck, Ludwik, 4, 10, 73, 74, 75
Foster, Johanna, 56, 75, 79, 82
Francis, Ara, 80
Freese, Lee, 76
Freud, Sigmund, 71, 85
Friedman, Asia, 28, 73, 75, 78, 80

García, Angela S., 84
Garfinkel, Harold, 8, 65, 74, 84

Geertz, Clifford, 73, 83
Germana, Rachelle, 56, 75, 79, 83
Glaser, Barney G., 18, 73, 74, 76, 77, 78, 79, 85
Goffman, Erving, 19, 27, 41, 61, 80
Gould, Roger V., 83, 84
Greenwald, David S., 77
Gricar, Julie M., 75

Haaken, Janice, 83
Hadamard, Jacques, 85
Hanemaayer, Ariane, 73
Hobsbawm, Eric, 48
Hochschild, Arlie, 27–28, 39, 78, 79
Hofstadter, Douglas, 40, 59, 71, 80, 81, 85
Holland, John, 81
Holyoak, Keith J., 79, 80, 85
Horwitz, Allan V., 76
Howard, Jenna, 56, 75, 83
Hughes, Everett C., 19, 41, 69, 76, 80, 84, 85

Isaacson, Nicole, 75

Jacobs, Jerry, 6, 73, 74
Jaffe-Dax, Tali, 79, 83
Jakobson, Roman, 50
James, William, 71, 85
Jordan, Mark, 77
Jutel, Annemarie, 77, 78, 84

Kadushin, Charles, 83
Kantorovich, Aharon, 74
Kennedy, Mary M., 78
Khong, Yuen F., 84
Kidahashi, Miwako, 75
Kitsuse, John I., 67, 84
Koestler, Arthur, 70–71, 83, 85
Koningsveld, Herman, 73
Kuhn, Thomas S., 74
Kuran, Timur, 78, 85

Leach, Edmund, 51, 81
Levine, Donald N., 76
Lévi-Strauss, Claude, 50, 81, 85
Lizardo, Omar, 83
Lofland, John, 76, 77, 78, 84
Lofland, Lyn H., 84
Luckmann, Thomas, 8, 14, 74, 75, 76

Malyk, Maria V., 75
Margalit, Avishai, 23, 77
Martin, John L., 44, 80
Mauss, Marcel, 44, 80
May, Ernest R., 84
McLean, Paul, 32, 79
McLuhan, Arthur, 76, 77, 78, 83
McRuer, Robert, 82
Mead, George H., 14, 76
Mead, Margaret, 82
Merton, Robert K., 4, 73
Meyer, Jan H. F., 73
Miller, Jonathan, 85
Mills, C. Wright, 75
Moody, James, 51, 81
Morrill, Calvin, 31, 78
Mullaney, Jamie L., 34, 56, 73, 75, 79, 82, 84

Naroll, Raoul, 30, 78
Neisser, Ulric, 74
Neustadt, Richard E., 84
Nippert-Eng, Christena E., 56, 73, 75, 79, 83

Papadantonakis, Max, 77, 82
Parsons, Talcott, 14, 76
Pasteur, Louis, 1, 7
Patterson, Orlando, 30, 78
Pearce, Richard M., 74
Peña-Alves, Stephanie, 75, 79, 83
Pike, Kenneth L., 50, 81
Pirkey, Melissa F., 83

Pirsig, Robert M., 60, 83
Poincaré, Henri, 78, 80
Pollock, Mica, 77
Ponticelli, Christy M., 51, 82
Proust, Marcel, 4, 73
Prus, Robert, 15, 76, 77, 78, 79,
    83, 84, 85
Puddephatt, Antony, 76, 77, 78, 83
Purcell, Kristen, 34, 75, 79, 82

Ragin, Charles C., 79
Reysen, Stephen, 51, 82
Rivera, Lauren A., 83
Rivera, Mark T., 76, 77
Roth, Julius A., 32, 79
Rothman, Barbara K., 51, 82
Ryan, Dan, 32, 79

Saeki, Eiko, 75
Saguy, Abigail C., 65, 67, 84
Sander, Emmanuel, 40, 59, 71,
    80, 81, 85
Saussure, Ferdinand de, 82
Schofield, Janet W., 88
Schutz, Alfred, 11, 75
Schwalbe, Michael, 76, 77, 79
Schwartz, Howard, 6, 73, 74
Simmel, Georg, 11, 14, 16–20, 29–30,
    33, 35, 40–41, 49, 73, 76, 77, 78, 79,
    80, 81, 84
Simpson, Ruth, 75
Skocpol, Theda, 48, 81
Smith, Gregory W. H., 76, 77, 85
Snow, David A., 76, 77, 79
Sorokin, Pitirim A., 10, 75
Spencer, Herbert, 44, 80
Spender, Dale, 83
Spitzer, Samantha, 56, 79, 82
Springborg, Robert, 48, 81
Stein, Karen, 75

Strauss, Anselm L., 74, 76,
    78, 79, 85
Stryker, Susan, 65, 84
Swedberg, Richard, 73
Swidler, Ann, 81

Tavory, Iddo, 44, 76, 80
Thagard, Paul, 79, 80, 85
Timmermans, Stefan, 76
Tracy, David, 83

Van den Hoonaard,
    Will C., 73
Van Gennep, Arnold, 44, 49,
    51, 80, 81
Vaughan, Diane, 41, 51, 73, 78, 80,
    81, 82, 85
Verhoeven, Jef C., 78

Wagner-Pacifici, Robin, 24, 78
Wajnryb, Ruth, 77
Ward, Anna, 67, 84
Watson, Ian, 75, 76, 79, 82
Waugh, Linda, 50
Weber, Max, 13, 34, 37, 65–66, 73,
    76, 79, 84
Weyland, Kurt, 48, 81
White, Douglas R., 51, 81
Whitehead, Andrew, 81
Winchester, Daniel, 44, 80
Wolfe, Deborah, 75
Wordsworth, William, 72

Yeh, Hsin-Yi, 75
Yonan, Joe, 84

Zeitlin, Steven J., 77
Zerubavel, Eviatar, 73, 74, 75, 76, 77,
    78, 79, 80, 81, 82, 83, 84, 85
Zerubavel, Yael, 78, 81, 83, 84

# Subject Index

abstraction, 15–16, 20
analogical transfers, 65–69
analogies, 40, 43–44, 47, 51, 53–54, 58, 60, 71–72
analogizing, 37–58, 64, 67, 72
analytical perspective, 5
*Ancestors and Relatives*, ix, 10, 21–22, 54, 61
applicability, 24–25. *See also* extrapolation
attention, 3, 5–6, 8–9, 11, 42–43, 63
  academic, 3–4, 14, 22, 70
attentional mentoring, 11. *See also* teaching
attentional socialization, 11–12, 43. *See also* teaching
awareness, 3, 48, 56, 58, 62, 64, 68–70

bisociation, 70–71
broad base of evidence, 26–28

cases, 13, 24, 26, 29, 32, 41, 55
chapters, 21
collecting data, 2–4, 6, 8–10, 18, 24–30, 39, 41
commonalities, 15, 19, 38–39, 41, 43–45, 63, 68, 71–72. *See also* similarity and difference
comparative research, 37–38, 41, 69
comparing, 30, 32, 37–39, 47–48, 51, 53, 55–56, 60, 65, 67, 69
concept-driven research, 3–6, 11–12, 20, 23–24
concept-driven sociology, ix, 6, 11–12, 15, 23–24, 36, 40, 64, 72
conception, 16

concepts, 3–4, 9–11, 16, 20, 24, 34, 40, 64–65, 67, 69
conceptual framework, 5–7, 19, 50, 62
conceptualizing, 16, 40
creativity, 71
cross-cultural analogizing, 43–47
cross-domain analogizing, 49–51, 53–56, 65–66
cross-historical analogizing, 47–48
cross-level analogizing, 57–58

data, 2–3, 10, 18–19, 23–30. *See also* collecting data
data-driven research, 2, 6
decontextualizing, 18, 20, 42, 62
dehistoricizing, 48
disattending disparities, 43, 56
disattending distinctness, 63
discovering, 4, 7, 16, 41, 48, 71
disregarding, 9, 61, 63, 72
  context, 40
  differences, 24, 40–43, 50–51, 53–55, 57–58, 63, 72
  distinctions, 15, 42, 48, 62
  scale, 18, 63
  variability, 43–44
distilling, 15, 19, 22, 62–63
diversity, 24–34
  contextual, 24–29
  cultural, 29–31
  historical, 30–31
  maximizing, 27–28
  situational, 31–34
downplaying distinctions, 44
downplaying singularity, 44

eclecticism, 27–28
epistemic readiness, 1, 7–9, 18, 40,
    43, 48, 50–51, 55, 57, 61, 71
Eureka moment, 71
examples, 23–27, 30, 32–34, 39,
    44–45, 54, 56
exampling, 23–36, 40
extrapolation, 23, 34, 64–67
eye opening, 4

focal coherence, 29–30
focal commitment, 6
focalizing concepts, 11
focus, 26
    conceptual, 6, 11–12
    proto-conceptual, 12
focused mind, 7–11, 60, 63
focusing, 1–12, 14, 20, 22, 43–45, 54,
    56, 62–63
formal commonality, 38, 57, 72
formal equivalence, 38–39, 41–42
formal features, 18, 20, 43
formal properties, 14, 20, 71

generalists, 30
generality, 17–18
generalizability, 13, 17, 25–28, 34
generalizing, 13–22, 25, 29
generic features, 44, 54, 69
genericity, 14, 19–22, 24–25, 30,
    37, 39, 62
genericizing, 15
generic properties, 27, 55, 63
generic sociology, ix, 13–19, 24–27,
    29–30, 38–40, 42–43, 47, 49, 62,
    67, 69, 71–72
grounded theory, 6

Hidden in Plain Sight, ix, 8–9, 42, 53
Hidden Rhythms, 25

ignoring, 5, 18, 63. See also
    disregarding

illustrating, 23–24, 26, 39
illustrations, 24, 27
imagination: analogical, 58
    sociological, 11
indexing, 20–21
instantiation, 14, 19, 24, 30, 40–41,
    43, 57, 61, 63, 70, 72
intellectual cross-fertilization, 62, 69
interest, 8, 15, 17, 26, 67–68

juxtaposing examples,
    30–31, 33–34

labeling, 43, 56, 64. See also naming
language, 43. See also naming
looking, 3–4, 11, 15, 17, 56
lumping, 40, 43, 56, 80n37

magnets, 3–4
mental access, 3–4, 62
mental fusion, 71
methodological no-nos, 63
methodological virtues, 63
methodology, 1, 7, 12, 25,
    27, 37, 59
multicase analysis, 24
multicontextual data, 25, 39
multicontextual exampling,
    29, 34, 37
multicontextuality, 25, 30
multidomain exampling, 32
multi-exampling, 25
multihistorical research, 30
multilevel research, 35–36
multiple-cultural
    research, 30, 44
multisituational analysis, 31–33

naming, 40, 46, 52
nonspecificity, 13–14. See also
    genericity
noticing, 3–4, 7–9, 42–43, 48–49, 51,
    56–57, 70

observations, 4–7, 9, 40, 61
overspecialization, 61

parallels, 30–31, 38–39, 41–58, 61–62,
    64–65, 67–70, 82n115
  cross-contextual, 68
  formal, 39, 42–43, 49–51, 55, 82
  historical, 47
particularity, 2, 6, 11, 13–20, 26,
    60–61, 67
patterns, 3–4, 7, 9, 15–17, 19, 22, 24–
    27, 29–31, 34, 38–39, 41, 43–44,
    46–48, 51, 54, 56–57, 61–63,
    67–68, 72
  analogous, 41–44, 48, 50–53, 55
  formal, 26, 39, 41, 48, 56, 63
  generic, 15–16, 19, 22, 24–26, 29,
    31, 34, 56, 61–63
  transcontextual, 25–26, 31,
    38, 61–63
  transcultural, 29–30, 44, 46–47
  transhistorical, 30, 47
Patterns of Time in Hospital Life, 8, 25
pre-ideas, 4. See also proto-ideas
proto-concepts, 4–5, 9, 12
proto-ideas, 4

reading, 8, 11–12, 15, 28, 45
research, 1–7, 11–12, 17, 22, 25–26,
    29, 41, 61
revealing, 3, 15, 20, 23, 25, 29–30,
    35, 37–39, 41, 44, 50–51, 54, 60,
    67–69, 72

sampling, 11, 24–28
selectivity, 5, 63–64
sensitivity, 4, 7–11, 71
  attentional, 3–4, 7–11, 55
sensitizing concepts, 3–5, 9–10
similarity and difference, 25–27, 38–
    41, 43, 48–51, 53, 55–59, 63–65,
    68, 71–72
Simmelarities, 41

socially patterned
  phenomena, 3, 15
Social Mindscapes, 10
social pattern analysis, 3, 15, 57
sociology, ix, 1–4, 6, 11–20, 22–23,
    34, 37, 41, 47, 55, 59, 64
structuralism, 50
students, ix, 1, 6, 11–12, 24, 34, 55, 64
surface and depth, 26, 59, 70–72

Taken for Granted, 7, 10, 20–21,
    33, 42, 54
teaching, 24–25, 34, 55. See also
    students
The Elephant in the Room, ix, 7, 9,
    20–21, 26, 31, 33, 53, 63
The Fine Line, ix, 4, 7, 19–20, 29, 33,
    42, 44, 51
themes, 21–22, 63
theoretical concerns, 6, 13, 17–18,
    20, 26, 29, 63
theoretically-driven research, 3
theoretical orientation, 6
theoretical relevance, 3–6, 9
theoretical sensitization, 8
theoretico-methodological agenda,
    ix, 19, 64
theoretico-methodological logic, 56
theoretico-methodological practices,
    23, 26, 38, 44, 48
theoretico-methodological
    tactics, 22, 63
theorizing: analogical, 40
  e.g.-style, 23
  formal, 14–15, 30, 35
  generic, 15, 19–22, 24, 30, 40, 55,
    57, 59, 62, 72
  sociological, 13–14, 41, 50, 67
  transcontextual, 21, 35, 59
theory, 1–2, 13, 30–31, 35, 60
Theory-driven research, 3
The Seven-Day Circle, 8, 44
thick analysis, 23, 26, 60

thinking analogically, 40, 49, 64, 70.
  *See also* analogizing
thinking cross-contextually, 37
thinking transcontextually, 61–62
*Time Maps*, ix, 7, 10, 19, 21, 26, 30,
  39, 44, 53, 62, 68
topics, 6–7, 21
transcending context, 18, 40
transcending singularity, 13–14,
  16, 61, 63
transcending specificity, 13–14,
  16–18, 20, 26
transcontextuality, ix, 18–21, 25, 34,
  37–39, 62, 66, 69, 72
transcontextual properties, 49,
  54–55, 63, 67

transcontextual research,
  17–19, 22, 68
transcultural research, 17, 20, 29
transdomain research, 18, 54
transhistorical research, 17, 20, 30
translevel research, 18
transsituational research, 18

uncovering, 38–39, 41–42, 44, 47–48,
  51, 54–57, 72
undergeneralizing, 60–61
uniformities, 17
universality, 10, 17

vocabulary, 9, 17, 65. *See also*
  language